Lecture Notes in Computer Science 16591

Founding Editors

Gerhard Goos
Juris Hartmanis

Editorial Board Members

Elisa Bertino, *Purdue University, West Lafayette, IN, USA*
Wen Gao, *Peking University, Beijing, China*
Bernhard Steffen, *TU Dortmund University, Dortmund, Germany*
Moti Yung, *Columbia University, New York, NY, USA*

The series Lecture Notes in Computer Science (LNCS), including its subseries Lecture Notes in Artificial Intelligence (LNAI) and Lecture Notes in Bioinformatics (LNBI), has established itself as a medium for the publication of new developments in computer science and information technology research, teaching, and education.

LNCS enjoys close cooperation with the computer science R & D community, the series counts many renowned academics among its volume editors and paper authors, and collaborates with prestigious societies. Its mission is to serve this international community by providing an invaluable service, mainly focused on the publication of conference and workshop proceedings and postproceedings. LNCS commenced publication in 1973.

Ana Nunes Alonso · Roberto Palmieri

Editors

Distributed Applications and Interoperable Systems

26th IFIP WG 6.1 International Conference, DAIS 2026
Held as Part of the 21st International Federated Conference
on Distributed Computing Techniques, DisCoTec 2026
Urbino, Italy, June 8–12, 2026, Proceedings

Editors
Ana Nunes Alonso
INESC TEC
Braga, Portugal

Roberto Palmieri
Lehigh University
Bethlehem, PA, USA

ISSN 0302-9743   ISSN 1611-3349 (electronic)
Lecture Notes in Computer Science
ISBN 978-3-032-27357-4   ISBN 978-3-032-27358-1 (eBook)
https://doi.org/10.1007/978-3-032-27358-1

This Springer imprint is published by the registered company Springer Nature Switzerland AG
The registered company address is: Gewerbestrasse 11, 6330 Cham, Switzerland

If disposing of this product, please recycle the paper.

Preface

This volume contains the papers presented at DAIS 2026: the 26th International Conference on Distributed Applications and Interoperable Systems, sponsored by the International Federation for Information Processing (IFIP). The DAIS conference series addresses all practical and conceptual aspects of distributed applications, including their design, modeling, implementation, and operation; the supporting middleware; appropriate software engineering methodologies and tools; and experimental studies and applications. DAIS 2026 was held from June 8–12, 2026, in Urbino, Italy, as part of DisCoTec 2026, the 21st International Federated Conference on Distributed Computing Techniques.

We offered three paper tracks: full research papers, full practical experience reports, and work-in-progress papers. We received 17 submissions: 16 were full papers, and one was a practical experience report (use-case paper). All submissions were single-blindly reviewed by at least three Program Committee (PC) members. The review process included a post-review discussion phase, during which the PC reviewed the merits of all papers. The committee decided to accept seven full research papers, for an acceptance rate of 43%. The accepted papers cover a broad range of topics in distributed computing, including modern applications.

The keynote at DAIS was delivered by Paolo Romano, from the Instituto Superior Técnico (IST) of the Universidade de Lisboa.

The conference was made possible by the hard work and cooperation of many people working in several different committees and organizations, all of which are listed in these proceedings. In particular, we are grateful to the PC members for their commitment and thorough reviews, and for their active participation in the discussion phase, and to all the external reviewers for their help in evaluating submissions. Finally, we also thank the DisCoTec General Chair, Claudio Antares Mezzina, and the DAIS Steering Committee Chair, Valerio Schiavoni, for their constant availability, support, and guidance.

June 2026

Ana Nunes Alonso
Roberto Palmieri

Organization

Program Committee Chairs

Ana Nunes Alonso   INESC TEC, Portugal
Roberto Palmieri   Lehigh University, USA

Steering Committee

Daniel Balouek   Inria, France
Silvia Bonomi   Università degli Studi di Roma "La Sapienza", Italy
Lydia Y. Chen   University of Neuchâtel, Switzerland
Frank Eliassen   University of Oslo, Norway
David Eyers   University of Otago, New Zealand
Rüdiger Kapitza   Friedrich-Alexander-Universität Erlangen-Nürnberg, Germany
Rolando Martins   University of Porto, Portugal
Miguel Matos   University of Lisboa & INESC-ID, Portugal
Ibéria Medeiros   University of Lisbon, Portugal
Marta Patino-Martínez   Technical University of Madrid, Spain
João Paulo   University of Minho, Portugal
Jose Pereira   University of Minho / INESC TEC, Portugal
Hans P. Reiser   Reykjavik University, Iceland
Anne Remke   University of Münster, Germany
Laura Ricci   University of Pisa, Italy
Etienne Riviére   UCLouvain, Belgium
Valerio Schiavoni (Chair)   University of Neuchâtel, Switzerland
Mennan Selimi   South East European University, North Macedonia
Spyros Voulgaris   Athens University of Economics and Business, Greece

Program Committee

Pierre Louis Aublin   IIJ Research Laboratory, Japan
Christian Berger   University of Passau, Germany

David Bermbach	TU Berlin, Germany
Cláudia Brito	INESC TEC, Portugal
Lorenzo Carnevale	University of Messina, Italy
Davide Frey	Inria, France
Ahmed Hassan	Lehigh University, USA
Pradeeban Kathiravelu	University of Alaska Anchorage, USA
João Leitão	Universidade Nova de Lisboa, Portugal
Odorico Machado Mendizabal	Federal University of Santa Catarina, Brazil
Sebastiano Peluso	Meta, USA
Etienne Riviére	UCLouvain, Belgium
Valerio Schiavoni	University of Neuchâtel, Switzerland
Lewis Tseng	University of Massachusetts Lowell, USA

Additional Reviewers

Paul Bergmann	Tim Christian Rese
Sebastian Koch	Trever Schirmer
Niklas Kowallik	Arne Vogel

Contents

Distributed Machine Learning

Storage and Distributed Systems

Distributed Machine Learning

Efficient Federated Search
for Retrieval-Augmented Generation Using
Lightweight Routing

Akash Dhasade[iD], Rachid Guerraoui[iD], Anne-Marie Kermarrec[iD],
Diana Petrescu[(✉)][iD], Rafael Pires[iD], Mathis Randl[iD], and Martijn de Vos[iD]

EPFL, Lausanne, Switzerland
`diana.petrescu@epfl.ch`

Abstract. Large language models (LLMs) achieve remarkable performance across domains but remain prone to hallucinations and inconsistencies. Retrieval-augmented generation (RAG) mitigates these issues by augmenting model inputs with relevant documents retrieved from external sources. In many real-world scenarios, relevant knowledge is fragmented across organizations or institutions, motivating the need for federated search mechanisms that can aggregate results from heterogeneous data sources without centralizing the data. We introduce RAGROUTE, a lightweight routing mechanism for federated search in RAG systems that dynamically selects relevant data sources at query time using a neural classifier, avoiding indiscriminate querying. This selective routing reduces communication overhead and end-to-end latency while preserving retrieval quality, achieving up to 80.65% reductions in communication volume and 52.50% reductions in latency across three benchmarks, while matching the accuracy of querying all sources.

Keywords: Retrieval-Augmented Generation · Large Language Models · Federated Search · Resource Selection · Routing

1 Introduction

Large language models (LLMs) have driven significant advancements across various domains such as natural language processing and healthcare [5,18,24]. Despite their widespread adoption, one major concern is their tendency to *hallucinate*, generating false responses with high confidence [20] and limiting their applicability in critical domains [21]. Retrieval-augmented generation (RAG) mitigates this issue by combining text generation with external retrieval, enhancing factual accuracy and contextual grounding [27,34].

Existing RAG systems typically rely on a single monolithic vector database [26]. In practice, however, real-world knowledge is often distributed across multiple heterogeneous information systems and repositories [6,39]. This setting calls for federated search, where queries are executed across multiple

© IFIP International Federation for Information Processing 2026
Published by Springer Nature Switzerland AG 2026
A. Nunes Alonso and R. Palmieri (Eds.): DAIS 2026, LNCS 16591, pp. 3–20, 2026.
https://doi.org/10.1007/978-3-032-27358-1_1

independent data sources and the results are merged into a unified ranking [36]. In RAG systems operating over multiple repositories, federated search constitutes the retrieval layer: queries are dispatched to selected data sources, their results are aggregated and reranked, and the resulting context is passed to the language model for generation. This avoids centralizing data, which might be complicated due to regulatory constraints or privacy considerations [8,23], and enables organizations to reuse existing infrastructure, therefore reducing operational and storage overhead.

A key challenge in federated search is resource selection [28,39], i.e., identifying which sources should be queried. Yet many RAG pipelines query all available resources [39]. Indiscriminate querying increases communication and computation costs [15] and may introduce irrelevant context that exacerbates hallucinations [7,10].

We introduce RAGROUTE, a novel and efficient routing mechanism for federated search in RAG systems that dynamically selects relevant data sources at query time using a lightweight neural network. By avoiding unnecessary queries, RAGROUTE significantly reduces resource consumption and end-to-end latency while maintaining high search quality. We evaluate RAGROUTE on three benchmarks: MIRAGE [42], MMLU [19] and FEB4RAG [39]. Our results show that RAGROUTE achieves up to 89.70% recall in source selection, reduces retrieval communication volume by up to 80.65%, and lowers end-to-end latency by up to 52.50%, while matching the accuracy of querying all data sources. This improvement stems primarily from reducing the number of documents that must be reranked during retrieval, thereby alleviating a major computational bottleneck in RAG pipelines.

In summary, our contributions are as follows:

1. We propose and implement RAGROUTE, a lightweight and effective routing mechanism for federated search in RAG that dynamically selects data sources per query, and make our code publicly available.[1]
2. We conduct extensive evaluations on three benchmarks, demonstrating that RAGROUTE significantly reduces communication overhead and latency while maintaining high retrieval quality and end-to-end accuracy.

2 Background and Problem Description

2.1 Retrieval-Augmented Generation (RAG)

RAG enhances the reliability of LLM responses by integrating external information as part of the input (or *prompt*) [27]. In a typical RAG pipeline, documents are split into chunks and encoded into dense vector embeddings, which are stored in a vector database that supports similarity search. For simplicity, we refer to document chunks as documents throughout this paper. Given a user query, the query is embedded using a compatible query encoder and a nearest-neighbor search is performed to retrieve the most relevant chunks. This search

---

[1] See https://github.com/sacs-epfl/ragroute.

is often accelerated using approximate nearest neighbor (ANN) indexing [29]. The retrieved candidates are commonly reranked and appended to the original query to form an augmented prompt for the LLM. By grounding generation in retrieved evidence, RAG reduces hallucinations and improves factual accuracy without requiring model retraining. Most existing RAG systems assume a single centralized vector database. In contrast, we consider settings where knowledge is distributed across multiple independent data sources, motivating federated search and resource selection.

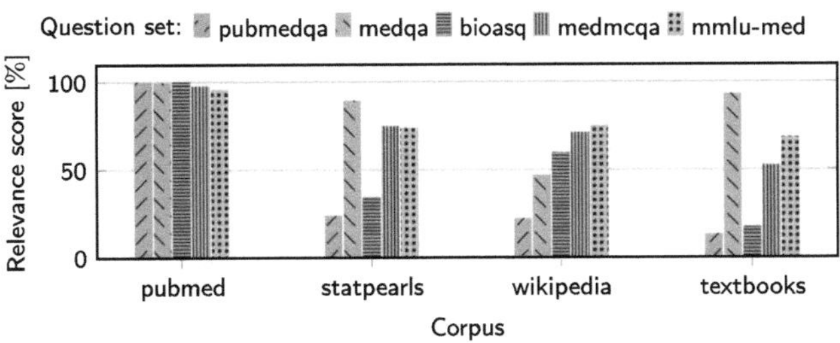

Fig. 1. The relevance of different corpora in RAG when answering questions, using question sets from the MIRAGE benchmark.

2.2 Towards Federated Search in RAG

Federated search is an information retrieval setting in which a query is executed across multiple independent data sources and the results are aggregated without centralizing the underlying data [36]. A key challenge in federated search is resource selection, i.e., determining which data sources should be queried [39]. In RAG systems operating over multiple repositories, source relevance varies substantially across queries, making accurate relevance estimation essential for efficient retrieval.

We empirically show this by analyzing data source relevance using corpora and questions from the MIRAGE benchmark (more details can be found in Sect. 4.1). This benchmark contains a large number of medical multiple-choice questions and answers and is divided into five question sets [42]. As knowledge backend for RAG we use four different data sources (corpora), namely PUBMED, STATPEARLS, WIKIPEDIA and TEXTBOOKS. For each question, we determine which corpora are relevant by considering a corpus relevant if at least one document originating from that corpus appears in the top-15 retrieved results.

Figure 1 shows the overall relevance of different corpora, highlighting how corpus usefulness varies across question sets. For example, the bar corresponding to the MEDQA question set and the STATPEARLS corpus shows a relevance score of 89.32%, meaning that for 89.32% of queries in MEDQA, at least one document in the retrieved relevant documents originates from STATPEARLS. While some corpora, such as PUBMED, consistently provide valuable, relevant information for all question sets, relying on a single corpus is often insufficient. Indeed, results from [42] demonstrate that combining multiple corpora improves retrieval performance. Some corpora, such as STATPEARLS or WIKIPEDIA, are only useful in particular cases. The TEXTBOOKS corpus, for example, is mostly irrelevant for the PUBMEDQA question set. The differences in corpus relevance motivate the importance of adequate resource selection for a given query.

One must strike a balance in the number of data sources being queried. While querying all available data sources guarantees full coverage, it also increases retrieval latency and computational overhead, as more requests, database searches, and document reranking operations are required. At the same time, under-selecting data sources risks missing critical information, particularly in domains where information is distributed sparsely across multiple repositories, for example, government data that resides in different portals [9]. Achieving a good trade-off between retrieval efficiency and response quality remains an open problem. Therefore, this work answers the following question: *how can we efficiently predict query-specific source relevance in federated search for RAG, while minimizing retrieval overhead?*

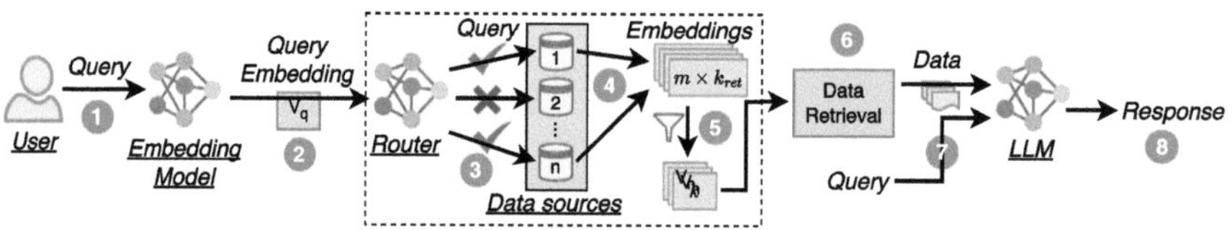

Fig. 2. The workflow of RAGROUTE. The components specific to RAGROUTE are indicated in the box with the dashed border.

3   Design of **RAGROUTE**

3.1   System Model and Assumptions

We assume a permissioned setting in which all data sources are known and trusted. Thus, we focus on federated search within an enterprise or institutional consortium. Each data source maintains its own data and associated local embeddings, and is responsible for computing and storing vector representations of its documents. The specifications of the embedding models used could vary across data sources. We assume that the enterprise or institution running the system has access to the embedding models used by the different data sources. User queries are submitted in natural language and converted into embedding vectors using the appropriate model(s). While we assume data sources are generally available, RAGROUTE remains functional even if some sources are temporarily offline. The system can simply exclude the offline data source from selection, ensuring graceful degradation in retrieval coverage rather than system failure.

3.2 RAGROUTE Workflow

We visualize the RAGROUTE workflow in Fig. 2, enabling RAG-enhanced LLM responses by retrieving documents from n distinct data sources. We show the components specific to RAGROUTE in the dashed box. When a user sends a query to the system ❶, the user query is first converted into one or more embeddings using all embedding models used by the data sources ❷. These query embeddings are then forwarded to a *router*, whose purpose is to decide which of the n data sources are relevant. The router predicts this relevance separately for each source using source specific features and query embeddings. We outline the design and operation of our router in Sect. 3.3.

After determining the m relevant data sources ($m \leq n$), we forward to each selected source the query embedding previously computed using its respective embedding model ❸. For example, Fig. 2 shows that data source 1 is selected and receives the query embedding, while source 2 is skipped. Each selected source uses the received query embedding to retrieve top-k_{ret} documents most similar to the query. This results in $m \times k_{ret}$ total retrieved documents ❹. This is followed by a post-retrieval reranking step, which has become a standard component in modern RAG systems [14,32,33]. Rerankers, often implemented as cross-encoder models, rescore the retrieved candidates to prioritize the passages most semantically relevant to the user query. This two-stage retrieval design improves grounding accuracy while also reducing response latency, since only a compact set of highly relevant documents is passed to the language model. After reranking, only final k documents are retained where the value of k can differ from the retrieval cutoff k_{ret} (see Sect. 4).

Finally, the relevant documents ❻ and original user query ❼ are combined into a single prompt. This prompt is fed to the LLM and a response is generated and returned to the user ❽, therefore completing the query.

3.3 Lightweight Query Routing

To enable resource selection and efficient retrieval across multiple data sources, RAGROUTE uses a lightweight query router, implemented as a shallow neural network (NN) with a few fully connected layers. This minimal design is intentional: the router must remain computationally inexpensive so that routing overhead is negligible compared to retrieval and generation. Despite its simplicity, the router is sufficient to estimate the relevance of each data source before retrieval. Using a shallow NN is inspired by practices in mixture of experts (MoE) models and ensembles. MoE models leverage a small router function to decide which subset of experts to activate [44]. Similarly, shallow NNs are used for decision-making in one-shot federated ensembles [3]. This work applies similar ideas to selecting relevant data sources in federated search for RAG systems. We next describe the training and inference phase of the RAGROUTE router.

Training Phase. Let $R = \{R_1, R_2, \ldots, R_n\}$ denote the set of n data sources, where each R_i corresponds to a collection of documents. For each query–source pair (q, R_i), the router estimates a relevance probability, which is thresholded to obtain a binary routing decision. The router is trained using ground-truth binary relevance labels $s(q, R_i) \in \{0, 1\}$, where $s(q, R_i) = 1$ indicates that source R_i is relevant to query q. We first describe how these ground-truth labels are constructed, before detailing the router input features. We consider two approaches for constructing the source-level relevance labels.

1. **Rerank based** – For a given query q, the top-k_{ret} documents are retrieved from each source $R_i \in R$. All retrieved documents are then reranked jointly using a neural reranker to produce a global top-k list. A source R_i is labeled as relevant if at least one retrieved document d from R_i appears in the global top-k:

$$s(q, R_i) = \begin{cases} 1 & \text{if } \exists \, d \in R_i \text{ s.t. } d \text{ is in the global top-}k \\ 0 & \text{otherwise.} \end{cases}$$

   These labels depend on both the embedding model and the value of k. During inference, we use the same value of k as for training.

2. **LLM based** [39] – For each query q, we first retrieve the the top-k_{ret} documents from each source $R_i \in R$. We then obtain query–document relevance judgments for these retrieved documents using an external LLM that is independent of the embedding model. Each document is assigned one of four labels: not relevant, minimally relevant, highly relevant, or key, where key indicates a strong match. For each source R_i, we aggregate the LLM judgments of its retrieved documents into a graded precision score:

$$\text{Graded Precision}(q, R_i) = \frac{\sum_{j=1}^{k} w(q, d_j)}{k} \times 100$$

   where d_j denotes the j-th retrieved document from source R_i for query q, and $w(q, d_j)$ is defined as:

$$w(q, d_j) = \begin{cases} 0 & \text{if not relevant} \\ 0.25 & \text{if minimally relevant} \\ 0.5 & \text{if highly relevant} \\ 1 & \text{if key.} \end{cases}$$

   Finally, a source is labeled as relevant if the Graded Precision score is positive:

$$s(q, R_i) = \begin{cases} 1 & \text{Graded Precision}(q, R_i) > 0 \\ 0 & \text{otherwise.} \end{cases}$$

   These labels depend only on the cutoff k_{ret} and not on the embedding model.

Feature Selection. While it is common to assume that each source uses the same embedding model to embed its documents [13], some specialized sources may instead employ their own embedding model [39]. We design our router to support the more general scenario where each source could have its own embedding model. Let $H_i(x) \in \mathbb{R}^{z_i}$ denote the embedding of any input x (a query or a document) using the embedding model of source R_i, where z_i is its embedding dimension. The router takes the following three features as input:

(i) the query embedding $H_i(q)$,
(ii) the centroid of the data source $C_i = \frac{1}{|R_i|} \sum_{d \in R_i} H_i(d)$, and
(iii) the source-id as one hot encoded vector Id_i.

The centroid C_i, computed as the average vector representation of all document embeddings in a data source, summarizes its overall semantic content. The source-id serves as a prior signal to help the router account for systematic differences across sources. Since the size of the embedding z_i may differ across sources, we consider the highest embedding size $z = \max_{i \in [n]} z_i$ and pad zeros if $z_i < z$. We denote the padded query embedding as $\hat{H}_i(q)$ and the padded centroid as $\hat{C}_i$, where $\hat{H}_i(q), \hat{C}_i \in \mathbb{R}^z$. The router parameterized by θ and denoted by f_θ independently predicts a relevance probability for each source $i \in [n]$ based on these features. Given a dataset of queries $\mathcal{D}_{\mathrm{train}}$ with ground truth relevance labels constructed as discussed before, the router is trained to minimize the following objective:

$$\mathcal{L}(\theta) = \sum_{q \in \mathcal{D}_{\mathrm{train}}} \sum_{i=1}^{n} \ell\left(f_\theta(\hat{H}_i(q), \hat{C}_i, \mathrm{Id}_i), \ s(q, R_i) \right) \tag{1}$$

where ℓ is a binary classification loss, such as binary cross-entropy.

Inference Phase. Once trained, RAGROUTE uses this model to efficiently route incoming user queries to relevant data sources. We run one forward pass for each of the available data sources individually to predict their relevance to a given inference query. This forward pass completes quickly (with sub-millisecond latency, see Sect. 4.3) and can be done in parallel for individual sources. Additionally, multiple queries can be batched into a single forward pass, depending on their arrival time. When new data sources are added or existing ones are updated, RAGROUTE regenerates the training ground truth by querying the affected sources together with those predicted as relevant by the existing router. This targeted querying strategy ensures that new and updated sources are incorporated into the label construction process while avoiding unnecessary queries to unrelated ones, thereby minimizing update overhead. Because the router is implemented as a shallow NN with only a few fully connected layers, retraining is highly lightweight, requiring minimal computation and storage. Thus, the router can be rapidly retrained in the background whenever updates occur.

4 Evaluation

4.1 Experimental Setup

Implementation. We implement RAGROUTE in Python using an event-driven architecture based on `asyncio`. Each core component (coordinator, router, data sources, and LLM engine) runs as an independent process to enable modularity and parallel execution. The coordinator orchestrates asynchronous communication across components. We use the ZeroMQ library for inter-process messaging and AIOHTTP to handle incoming HTTP queries. We use the Ollama framework for inference which provides a convenient way to load and run inference with different LLMs [31]. For the embedding models, we use the PyTorch library.

Router Model. We implement the router as a lightweight fully connected NN. The network consists of hidden layers with 128, 64, and 32 neurons, each followed by Layer Normalization, ReLU activation, and Dropout to improve stability and prevent overfitting. These hyperparameters were selected through cross-validation, where we evaluated several architectures with varying numbers of layers and hidden dimensions on the validation set. The output layer consists of a single neuron that produces a raw logit score, predicting whether the corpus is relevant to the given query. The model is trained using Binary Cross-Entropy with Logits Loss with a positional weight to address class imbalance. We use a cyclic scheduler for the learning rate γ, oscillating γ between 0.001 and 0.005. Model performance is evaluated on the validation set after each epoch, and the best model is selected based on validation accuracy. Training data are split by question into 30%/10%/60% train/validation/test partitions, and all input features are standardized using a StandardScaler. The router's small size ensures fast training, negligible inference overhead, and ease of retraining when data sources evolve. We also tested alternative classifiers (*e.g.*, logistic regression and random forests) but found the shallow NN performed best overall.

Datasets. We evaluate RAGRoute with the following three benchmarks:

(*i*) **MIRAGE** is a benchmark designed to evaluate RAG systems for medical question answering [42]. It consists of 7663 questions drawn from five widely used medical QA datasets. We use MedRAG as knowledge source, which includes four corpora with documents related to healthcare [42]. For generating embeddings, we use MedCPT [22], a domain-specific model designed for biomedical contexts. For retrieval, we use the IndexFlatL2 index structure, provided by the FAISS library [12], ensuring exact search and eliminating sources of approximation in our experiments. We treat each corpus as a separate data source. For MIRAGE, we construct the ground truth relevance labels using the rerank based approach. To run RAGRoute with a RAG pipeline, we leverage the code provided by the MedRAG toolkit.

(*ii*) **MMLU** is a benchmark that evaluates LLM systems across tasks ranging from elementary mathematics to legal reasoning [19]. For our experiments, we use eight subject-specific subsets of MMLU with a total of 2803 questions. As a knowledge source, we use a Wikipedia dataset [25]. From this dataset, we cluster the documents into ten groups using the k-means algorithm to simulate different data sources. After clustering, we observe variance in the cluster size, ranging from 1.41 M to 2.88 M vectors per cluster. For MMLU, we construct the ground truth relevance labels using the rerank based approach. To run MMLU, we leverage the code provided by the RQABENCH framework [37].

(*iii*) **FEB4RAG** is a benchmark designed to evaluate federated search methods for RAG systems [39]. It consists of 790 user queries spanning diverse domains and complexity levels. FEB4RAG is derived from BEIR [38] and includes 13 heterogeneous data sources powered by eight distinct embedding models, enabling evaluation under realistic federated retrieval settings. For FEB4RAG, ground truth relevance labels are obtained using the LLM based approach. Unlike MIRAGE and MMLU, FEB4RAG does not provide verifiable ground-truth answers.

Evaluation. To facilitate automated evaluation, we developed a separate benchmarking script that iterates over all questions in a given dataset and sends each query, along with the associated answer choices if applicable, to the RAGROUTE system via HTTP requests. Queries are sent one by one: the script waits for the response to a given query before proceeding to the next. Upon receiving a response from the system, the script verifies the correctness of the answer against the ground truth answer, if applicable. This setup enables systematic and reproducible evaluation across multiple benchmarks.

Retrieval and Reranking. For all datasets, we retrieve a global top-$k = 15$ list of documents for generation. To construct this final set, each selected data source retrieves top-$k_{ret} = 50$ documents most similar to the query using exact similarity search with FAISS [12] incurring negligible latency compared to the reranker. We set k_{ret} sufficiently large to ensure high recall, while balancing the trade-off with reranking cost. All retrieved candidates are then reranked to produce the global top-15 list. This two-stage retrieval strategy balances recall and precision: a sufficiently large retrieval pool ensures coverage, while reranking improves semantic relevance and reduces noise in the final context. We employ the `BAAI/bge-reranker-v2-m3` model [1], a lightweight cross-encoder reranker designed for multilingual reranking with efficient inference.

LLM Models. As LLM, we use the open-source LLaMA 3.1 8B Instruct model for all above datasets [17] as it is commonly considered in related work [2, 35]. We adopt a zero-shot chain-of-thought prompting scheme, instructing the model to reason step-by-step before providing the final answer. The output is formatted in JSON to ensure interpretable reasoning and structured evaluation.

Hardware. We run our experiments on a compute cluster equipped with an NVIDIA A100 GPU for LLM answer generation, and 500 GB of main memory.

Routing baselines. To analyze the effectiveness and efficiency of RAGROUTE, we experiment with the following four routing strategies.

(*i*) **NONE.** This routing strategy does not query any data source and the input prompt to the LLM is not enhanced with retrieved documents.

(*ii*) **ALL.** Under this routing strategy, all data sources are queried. This can be considered as a naive baseline for federated search that lacks a mechanism for strategic resource selection.

Table 1. Classification metrics (averages) for our router and for different benchmarks. RAGRoute router achieves high accuracy and recall, demonstrating good generalization across benchmarks.

Benchmark	Accuracy (%)	Precision (%)	Recall (%)	F1-Score (%)	AUC (%)
MIRAGE	86.63	86.79	83.35	84.96	92.94
MMLU	90.93	71.64	82.92	76.87	95.77
FeB4RAG	83.05	87.37	89.70	88.51	84.00

(iii) **RAGRoute.** This routing strategy uses the RAGRoute router to identify and retrieve documents only from relevant data sources.

(iv) **RANDOM.** This routing strategy randomly selects a fixed number of data sources, matching the number selected by RAGRoute but without using relevance predictions. We incorporate this strategy to evaluate the effectiveness of RAGRoute beyond extremes like querying all or no data sources. This allows us to ignore the effect of the number of contacted sources, isolating the impact of how the sources are selected, demonstrating that RAGRoute gains arise from intelligent, query-aware routing.

Metrics. Our experiments primarily focus on the classification performance of the RAGRoute router model and the system efficiency of the entire RAGRoute system. For the former, we report standard classification metrics such as accuracy, recall, precision, F1-Score and AUC. For the latter, we monitor, for each user query, relevant system metrics such as the number of data sources contacted, communication volume and latency. We also determine the end-to-end RAG accuracy for the MMLU and MIRAGE benchmarks. We are unable to do so for FeB4RAG since this benchmark does not provide ground-truth answers.

4.2   RAGRoute Routing Effectiveness

We evaluate the effectiveness of our router and show its classification performance in predicting data source relevance for a given query in the test set for each benchmark. Table 1 presents various classification metrics, *i.e.*, accuracy, precision, recall, F1-score, and AUC, for all three benchmarks. Here, recall measures the router's ability to identify all relevant data sources, while accuracy reflects the overall correctness of the router's binary predictions (and not the end-to-end LLM accuracy in generating final responses).

We achieve consistently strong results across all benchmarks, with accuracy ranging from 83.05% for FeB4RAG to 90.93% for MMLU, and recall values between 89.70% and 82.92% respectively, indicating that the router reliably identifies relevant data sources across diverse settings. The slightly lower accuracy on some benchmarks primarily stems from our design choice to favor recall which is particularly important for imbalanced datasets where only a few sources are relevant per query. This trade-off is desirable in federated retrieval settings, where missing a relevant data source is typically more detrimental to the quality of LLM answers than querying an additional one. Overall, the RAGROUTE router demonstrates strong and balanced generalization across benchmarks, confirming its effectiveness for real-world federated search in RAG systems.

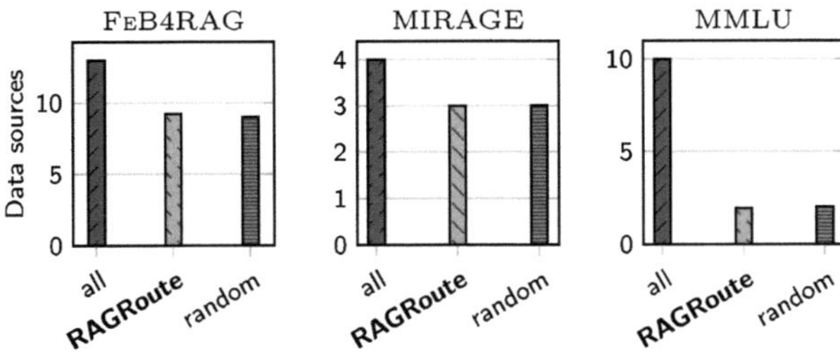

Fig. 3. The average number of queries (data sources contacted) for all benchmarks and for different routing strategies. RAGROUTE significantly reduces the number of contacted data sources compared to ALL baseline.

4.3   RAGROUTE Efficiency Gains

We now quantify the reduction by RAGROUTE in the number of data sources contacted and communication volume related to document retrieval for all routing baselines. We also analyze the end-to-end RAG accuracy and provide a time breakdown of different operations in the RAG workflow.

Number of Data Sources Contacted. Figure 3 shows the total number of data sources contacted across all queries, for all routing strategies and benchmarks. We find that the number of data sources contacted for the RAGROUTE routing strategy is always lower compared to querying all data sources (which is the ALL routing strategy). This effect is the most pronounced on the MMLU dataset, where the number of contacted data sources decreases from 16 810 to 3250, representing an *80.67% reduction* in the number of messages exchanged for document retrieval. In other words, under the RAGROUTE routing strategy, only 1.93 out of ten data sources are contacted on average. On average, RAGROUTE contacts 2.98 out of four data sources per query on MIRAGE, and 9.20 out of thirteen on FEB4RAG. These results highlight the effectiveness of RAGROUTE in minimizing communication and computation overhead during federated retrieval, while maintaining high routing accuracy.

Communication Volume. We next show the reduction in communication volume achieved by querying only relevant data sources. By selecting a subset of sources predicted as relevant, RAGROUTE significantly decreases the communication volume between the coordinator and data sources. Figure 4 (left column) reports the total communication volume for the three routing strategies:

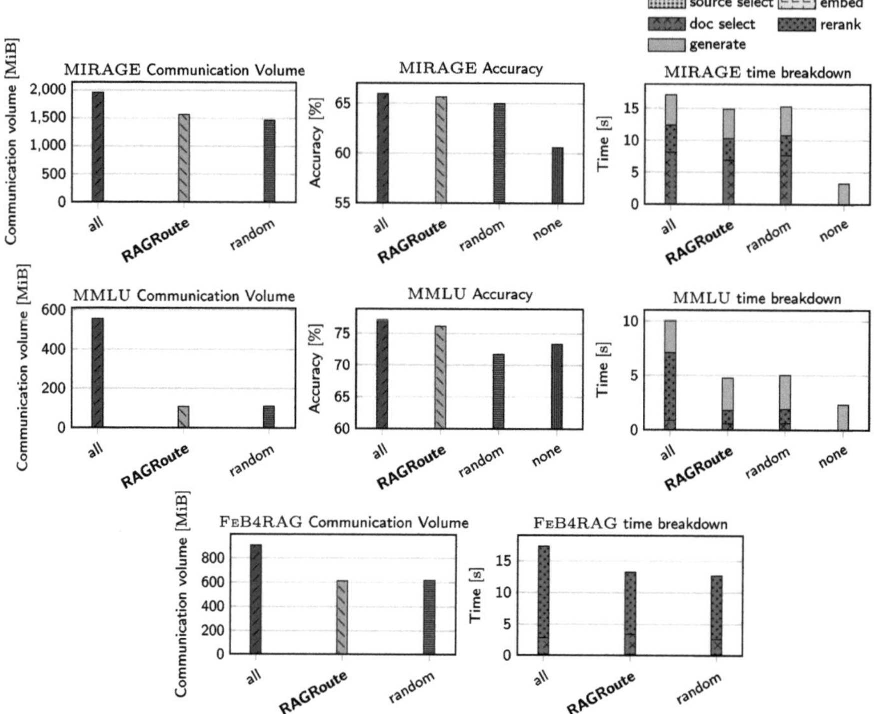

Fig. 4. The communication volume required for document retrieval (left), RAG test accuracy (middle) and query time breakdown (right), for all routing strategies and benchmarks. RAGRoute consistently reduces communication volume and maintains near-optimal accuracy, with improved query latency.

ALL, RAGRoute, and RANDOM. Compared to the ALL baseline, RAGRoute reduces total communication volume by 19.94% (1955.4 MiB → 1565.4 MiB) on MIRAGE, by 80.65% (554.4 MiB → 107.3 MiB) on MMLU, and by 32.52% (905.3 MiB → 610.9 MiB) on FeB4RAG. The RANDOM baseline, which queries a similar number of sources as RAGRoute, also lowers communication volume compared to ALL, but at the cost of lower accuracy, as shown next.

End-to-End RAG Accuracy. Finally, we report the average end-to-end accuracy on the MIRAGE and MMLU benchmarks. For the FeB4RAG benchmark, this metric is omitted, as no ground-truth answers are available to evaluate the correctness of generated outputs.

Figure 4 (middle column) shows the end-to-end accuracy results. On the MMLU benchmark, RAGRoute achieves an average accuracy of 76.09%, nearly matching the ALL baseline (77.10%). In contrast, the RANDOM baseline reaches only 71.74%, underperforming even the NONE baseline (73.35%). This drop illustrates the negative impact of indiscriminate retrieval: introducing irrelevant or noisy documents can distract the language model and ultimately reduce answer quality. By contrast, RAGRoute's selective routing ensures that documents only from relevant sources contribute to the answer quality.

On the MIRAGE benchmark, the NONE baseline achieves 60.58% accuracy, while randomly querying data sources increases it to 64.98%. When the data sources are selected via RAGRoute, accuracy further improves to 65.64%, closely matching the ALL baseline at 66.96%. Overall, RAGRoute maintains nearly optimal RAG accuracy while greatly reducing communication volume.

Time Breakdown. We further explore the efficiency gains of RAGRoute and provide for each dataset a time breakdown when answering a user query. These results are shown in Fig. 4 (right column) for each of the routing baselines, and we measure the time spent in the following five components. SOURCE SELECTION refers to the time spent on the inference request of the RAGRoute router, which predicts the set of relevant data sources for a given query. EMBEDDING denotes the time required to compute the query embeddings using the appropriate embedding models for all data sources. DOC SELECTION measures the time elapsed from when the coordinator dispatches the query to the selected data sources until all retrieval results are received. This includes network communication, client-side retrieval, and result transmission. RERANK represents the time consumed by the reranker to rescore and reorder the retrieved candidates, producing the global top-k set of documents. Finally, GENERATE corresponds to the time required by the LLM to synthesize the final response given the reranked context documents and user query. The SOURCE SELECTION, EMBEDDING, DOC SELECTION, and RERANK times are zero for the NONE routing baseline, as no data sources are queried in this configuration. For the FEB4RAG benchmark, we report only the SOURCE SELECTION, EMBEDDING, DOC SELECTION, and RERANK times, since no ground-truth answers are available to evaluate the GENERATE phase.

We first observe that the end-to-end query latency of RAGRoute varies across datasets, reflecting differences in corpus scale. When using the RAGRoute routing strategy, queries complete on average in 14.91 s on MIRAGE and 4.75 s on MMLU. These variations are explained by two factors. First, MIRAGE contains larger and more textually rich corpora, increasing the time needed to fetch and process documents. Second, the number of tokens included in the LLM input prompt is approximately twice as high for MIRAGE compared to MMLU, resulting in longer generation times (4.63 s vs. 2.96 s). For FEB4RAG, the query answer latency averages around 13.21 s, but this value excludes generation time because no verifiable ground-truth answers are available for this dataset.

An interesting observation is that reranking is a major contributor to overall latency. For example, in the ALL baseline, reranking alone accounts for 6.27 s on MMLU (around 62.64% of total latency) and 14.49 s on FEB4RAG (around 83.90% of the retrieval pipeline, excluding generation), showing that the cross-encoder reranker can become a major computational bottleneck in RAG systems operating over multiple data sources, as the number of considered sources grows. In contrast, RAGROUTE effectively mitigates this bottleneck by fetching documents from fewer sources, effectively reducing the number of candidate documents that must be reranked. With RAGROUTE, reranking time decreases by 80.70% on MMLU (from 6.27 s to 1.21 s) and by 32.51% on FEB4RAG (from 14.49 s to 9.78 s). Importantly, this reranking cost reduction directly translates into faster end-to-end query execution, without compromising retrieval accuracy or grounding quality.

Meanwhile, the latency overhead of pre-retrieval components (embedding generation and routing inference) is almost negligible. Even for FEB4RAG, where the query must be embedded multiple times using different models, the overall embedding and routing time remains imperceptible on the figure. In standalone inference measurements with a batch size of 32, the router imposes an average latency of only 0.4 ms using an NVIDIA A100 GPU and 0.8 ms using an AMD EPYC 7543 32-Core CPU. This highlights that the routing step performed by RAGROUTE adds negligible computational overhead and has an insignificant impact on the end-to-end query latency. Overall, these results show that the pre-retrieval routing in RAGROUTE significantly alleviates the reranking bottleneck while adding almost no overhead. Our design enables scalable, low-latency federated retrieval even when the number of data sources grows.

4.4   Ablation Study

We conduct an ablation study to evaluate the contribution of different input features to the router's performance on the MIRAGE and FEB4RAG benchmarks. Specifically, we train the router to predict relevance using the following combinations of features: *(i)* the query embedding and the centroid, *(ii)* the query embedding and the source-id, and *(iii)* all three features (Sect. 3.3). The query embedding must always be present as an input feature to be able to predict relevance for that query. Table 2 summarizes the results. The model trained with all three features achieves the highest recall on both the MIRAGE and FEB4RAG benchmarks, indicating that both the centroid and the source-id are important for effective routing. We also explored additional features such as the number of documents per source and the density around the centroid. However, including these features did not lead to further performance improvements.

Table 2. Ablation study of router's input features. Using all three features results in the highest performance on both benchmarks.

query	centroid	source-id	Recall	
			MIRAGE	FEB4RAG
✓	✓	✗	81.53	89.07
✓	✗	✓	82.33	88.33
✓	✓	✓	**83.35**	**89.70**

5   Related Work

RAG with Multiple Data Sources. FEB4RAG examines federated search within the RAG paradigm and focuses on optimizing resource selection and result merging to enhance retrieval efficiency [39]. The underlying idea consists of introducing a dataset for federated search and incorporating LLM-based relevance judgments to benchmark resource selection strategies. Notably, the paper emphasizes the importance of developing novel federated search strategies for RAG. Salve et al. propose a multi-agent RAG system where different agents handle the querying of databases with differing data formats (*e.g.*, relational or NoSQL) [35].

Other approaches focus on privacy in federated search. RAFFLE is a framework that integrates RAG into the federated learning pipeline and leverages public datasets during training while using private data only at inference time [30]. C-FEDRAG is a federated RAG approach that enables queries across multiple data sources and leverages hardware-based trusted execution environments (TEEs) to ensure data confidentiality [2]. FRAG leverages homomorphic encryption to enable parties to collaboratively perform ANN searches on encrypted query vectors and data stored in distributed vector databases, ensuring that no party can access others' data or queries [43]. These schemes can benefit from RAGROUTE while ensuring privacy-preserving federated search.

Machine Learning (ML)-Assisted Resource Selection. ML models have been explored to support resource selection in federated search [16]. Arguello *et al.* leverage different features, *e.g.*, the topic of queries, and train a classifier for resource selection [4]. Learn-to-rank approaches such as SVMRANK [11] and the LambdaMART-based LTRRS [41] refine relevance rankings by leveraging diverse feature sets. Ergashev *et al.* construct a heterogeneous graph to capture query-source and source-source relationships and then predict the query-source relevance ranking using a graph neural network (GNN) [13]. Wang *et al.* use an LLM as a resource selector, introducing a novel prompting approach called ReSLLM [40]. They also propose to fine-tune ReSLLM through previously logged queries and snippets from data sources. However, these approaches are either more computationally expensive than the lightweight RAGROUTE router or cannot handle heterogeneous embedding models across data sources.

6   Conclusion

We presented RAGROUTE, a novel and efficient routing mechanism for federated search in RAG systems. By dynamically choosing relevant data sources at query time via a lightweight neural classifier, RAGROUTE minimizes unnecessary queries while preserving high retrieval quality. Evaluations on MIRAGE, MMLU, and FEB4RAG demonstrate that RAGROUTE reduces the number of contacted sources and document retrieval communication volume by up to 80.65%, and decreases end-to-end latency by up to 52.50%, with minimal impact on end-to-end accuracy. These gains are primarily achieved by reducing reranking overhead which constitutes a major bottleneck in RAG pipelines. Our results confirm that querying all data sources is often unnecessary, underscoring the importance of query-aware retrieval strategies in federated search workflows for RAG.

Acknowledgments. This work has been co-funded by the Swiss National Science Foundation under the project *FRIDAY: Frugal, Privacy-Aware and Practical Decentralized Learning*, SNSF proposal No. 10.001.796.

References

1. Baai/bge-reranker-v2-m3. https://huggingface.co/BAAI/bge-reranker-v2-m3
2. Addison, P., Nguyen, M.T.H., et al.: C-FedRAG: a confidential federated retrieval-augmented generation system. arXiv preprint arXiv:2412.13163 (2024)
3. Allouah, Y., Dhasade, A., et al.: Revisiting ensembling in one-shot federated learning. In: NeurIPS (2025)
4. Arguello, J., Callan, J., Diaz, F.: Classification-based resource selection. In: CIKM (2009)
5. Bharathi Mohan, G., Prasanna Kumar, R., et al.: An analysis of large language models: their impact and potential applications. Knowl. Inf. Syst. (2024)
6. Bhavnani, S.K., Wilson, C.S.: Information scattering. In: Encyclopedia of Library and Information Sciences (2009)
7. Bian, N., Lin, H., et al.: Influence of external information on large language models mirrors social cognitive patterns. IEEE Trans. Comput. Soc. Syst. (2025)
8. Callan, J.: Distributed information retrieval. In: Advances in Information Retrieval: Recent Research from the Center for Intelligent Information Retrieval (2002)
9. Clifton, C.: Federated search (2016). https://www.cs.purdue.edu/homes/clifton/cs54701/FederatedSearch_0310.pdf
10. Cuconasu, F., Trappolini, G., et al.: The power of noise: redefining retrieval for RAG systems. In: SIGIR (2024)
11. Dai, Z., Kim, Y., Callan, J.: Learning to rank resources. In: SIGIR (2017)
12. Douze, M., Guzhva, A., et al.: The FAISS library. IEEE Trans. Big Data (2025)
13. Ergashev, U., Dragut, E., Meng, W.: Learning to rank resources with GNN. In: WWW (2023)
14. Gao, Y., Xiong, Y., et al.: Retrieval-augmented generation for large language models: a survey. arXiv preprint arXiv:2312.10997 (2024)
15. Garba, A., Khalid, S., Ullah, I., Khusro, S., Mumin, D.: Embedding based learning for collection selection in federated search. Data Technol. Appl. (2020)
16. Garba, A., Wu, S., Khalid, S.: Federated search techniques: an overview of the trends and state of the art. Knowl. Inf. Syst. (2023)
17. Grattafiori, A., Dubey, A., et al.: The LLaMA 3 herd of models. arXiv preprint arXiv:2407.21783 (2024)
18. Haltaufderheide, J., Ranisch, R.: The ethics of chatGPT in medicine and healthcare: a systematic review on large language models (LLMs). NPJ Digit. Med. (2024)

19. Hendrycks, D., Burns, C., et al.: Measuring massive multitask language understanding. arXiv preprint arXiv:2009.03300 (2021)
20. Ji, Z., Lee, N., et al.: Survey of hallucination in natural language generation. ACM Comput. Surv. (2023)
21. Ji, Z., Yu, T., et al.: Towards mitigating LLM hallucination via self reflection. In: Findings of EMNLP (2023)
22. Jin, Q., Kim, W., et al.: MedCPT: contrastive pre-trained transformers with large-scale PubMed search logs for zero-shot biomedical information retrieval. Bioinformatics (2023)
23. Kairouz, P., McMahan, H.B., et al.: Advances and open problems in federated learning. Found. Trends Mach. Learn. (2021)
24. Kaplan, J., McCandlish, S., et al.: Scaling laws for neural language models. arXiv preprint arXiv:2001.08361 (2020)
25. Karpukhin, V., Oguz, B., et al.: Dense passage retrieval for open-domain question answering. In: EMNLP (2020)
26. Kukreja, S., Kumar, T., et al.: Performance evaluation of vector embeddings with retrieval-augmented generation. In: ICCCS (2024)
27. Lewis, P., Perez, E., et al.: Retrieval-augmented generation for knowledge-intensive NLP tasks. In: NeurIPS (2020)
28. Li, L., Zhang, Z., Wu, S.: LDA-based resource selection for results diversification in federated search. In: WISA (2018)
29. Li, W., Zhang, Y., et al.: Approximate nearest neighbor search on high dimensional data–experiments, analyses, and improvement. IEEE Trans. Knowl. Data Eng. (2020)
30. Muhamed, A., Thaker, P., et al.: Cache me if you can: the case for retrieval augmentation in federated learning. In: ICLR Workshop on Privacy Regulation and Protection in Machine Learning (2024)
31. Ollama: Ollama: get up and running with large language models. GitHub repository (2025). https://github.com/ollama/ollama. Accessed 18 Feb 2025
32. OpenAI Cookbook: Search reranking with cross-encoders (2024). https://cookbook.openai.com/examples/search_reranking_with_cross-encoders
33. Pinecone: Refine with Rerank: Better RAG results using cross-encoders (2024). https://www.pinecone.io/learn/refine-with-rerank/
34. Şakar, T., Emekci, H.: Maximizing rag efficiency: a comparative analysis of RAG methods. Natural Lang. Process. (2025)
35. Salve, A., Attar, S., et al.: A collaborative multi-agent approach to retrieval-augmented generation across diverse data. arXiv preprint arXiv:2412.05838 (2024)
36. Shokouhi, M., Si, L.: Federated search. Found. Trends Inf. Retr. (2011)
37. Team, M.: Retrieval-QA-benchmark: a benchmark for evaluating retrieval-augmented QA systems (2024). https://github.com/myscale/Retrieval-QA-Benchmark
38. Thakur, N., Reimers, N., et al.: BEIR: a heterogeneous benchmark for zero-shot evaluation of information retrieval models. In: NeurIPS Datasets and Benchmarks (2021)
39. Wang, S., Khramtsova, E., Zhuang, S., Zuccon, G.: FeB4RAG: evaluating federated search in the context of retrieval augmented generation. In: SIGIR (2024)
40. Wang, S., Zhuang, S., et al.: ReSLLM: large language models are strong resource selectors for federated search. In: WWW Companion (2025)
41. Wu, T., Liu, X., Dong, S.: LTRRS: a learning to rank based algorithm for resource selection in distributed information retrieval. In: CCIR (2019)

42. Xiong, G., Jin, Q., et al.: Benchmarking retrieval-augmented generation for medicine. In: Findings of ACL (2024)
43. Zhao, D.: FRAG: toward federated vector database management for collaborative and secure retrieval-augmented generation. arXiv preprint arXiv:2410.13272 (2024)
44. Zhou, Y., Lei, T., et al.: Mixture-of-experts with expert choice routing. In: NeurIPS (2022)

HyperCluster: Decentralized Large Language Model Inference over Peer-to-Peer Wireless Networks

P. Samarth[(✉)], Vyoman Jain, Sanjiv Raghunandan, Akepati Ramya Sri, and Richa Sharma

Department of Computer Science, PES University, Bengaluru, India
{PES2UG22CS495,PES2UG22CS672,PES2UG22CS045,
PES2UG22CS504}@pesu.pes.edu, richasharma@pes.edu

Abstract. The substantial memory and computational requirements of large language models (LLMs) hinder their deployment on individual resource-constrained devices. This paper introduces HyperCluster, a framework for fully decentralized collaborative inference over peer-to-peer wireless networks. HyperCluster presents three core innovations: (1) a ring-based pipelined inference protocol where nodes deterministically self-organize into a computational ring based on device capabilities and pass intermediate states directly between peers via QUIC-based direct transport; (2) a generalizable model sharding methodology built on top of the Hugging Face Transformers library that automatically partitions any dense LLM across heterogeneous devices according to available memory; (3) selective layer loading from safetensors files, which only loads the tensor weights required by each node's assigned shard. We validate HyperCluster on a heterogeneous cluster of consumer-grade devices, demonstrating distributed inference of models up to 3 billion parameters with comprehensive latency and throughput analysis across one to three node configurations.

Keywords: Distributed AI · Peer-to-Peer Networks · LLM Inference · Model Sharding

1 Introduction

The proliferation of large language models (LLMs) has created unprecedented need for computational resources. State of the art models require tens to hundreds of gigabytes of memory, that far exceed the capacity of typical consumer and edge devices. Accessing these models through cloud services introduces privacy concerns, increases reliance on centralized infrastructure, and has costs associated with every usage. To overcome these barriers, we envision a truly decentralized alternative which enables users in resource-constrained environments to pool everyday devices—such as standard laptops over a wireless network—to collectively run multi-billion parameter models without relying on the cloud.

A. Nunes Alonso and R. Palmieri (Eds.): DAIS 2026, LNCS 16591, pp. 21–35, 2026.
https://doi.org/10.1007/978-3-032-27358-1_2

An alternative paradigm is **collaborative inference**, where multiple devices in a peer-to-peer (P2P) network pool their resources to collectively execute a model that is too large for any single device [9]. However, realizing this vision in a decentralized wireless environment presents significant challenges. Frameworks designed for distributed training in data centers, such as Megatron-LM [13] and DeepSpeed [12], depend on high-bandwidth, low-latency interconnects and stable cluster memberships which are assumptions that do not hold in dynamic P2P networks. Existing distributed inference systems [1,2,6,8] require centralized coordination, are restricted to local networks, or lack broad model compatibility.

This paper introduces HyperCluster, a framework for fully decentralized collaborative inference designed specifically for heterogeneous devices over P2P networks across the internet. We make the following contributions:

1. **Decentralized Ring-Pipeline Protocol:** A coordinator-free inference protocol where nodes self-organize into a deterministic computational ring, based on their advertised memory capacities. QUIC [7] based direct transport mechanism is used for low-latency tensor forwarding and pre-warmed connections to eliminate setup overhead.
2. **Generalizable Transformers-Based Sharding Engine:** A dynamic model sharding system which is built upon the Hugging Face Transformers library [18]. This allows us to automatically partition dense, off-the-shelf LLMs across heterogeneous devices, based on the available memory on each device, without requiring any model-specific modifications.
3. **Selective Layer Loading:** A memory-efficient model loading strategy that creates an empty model skeleton, and then loads only the tensors required by each node's assigned shard directly from safetensors [5] files. Along with this, we use a weight tying preservation mechanism to correctly handle models with tied embedding weights (e.g., small models like Llama-3.2 [4], Qwen3 0.6B [19]).

We validate HyperCluster on a heterogeneous cluster of consumer-grade devices, providing detailed latency breakdown, throughput analysis, and memory efficiency measurements across multiple model families and cluster configurations.

2   Background and Related Work

This research builds upon two primary domains: (1) large-scale parallel systems designed for centralized data centers, and (2) emerging frameworks for decentralized, peer-to-peer computation.

2.1   Model Parallelism in Centralized Environments

The challenge of partitioning large neural models has been thoroughly investigated within data center environments. Megatron-LM [13] and DeepSpeed [12] introduced foundational techniques for distributing models across multiple GPUs, while Alpa [21] refined these with automated inter- and intra-operator parallelism. However, these systems assume stable hardware, high-bandwidth interconnects (e.g., NVLink, InfiniBand), and homogeneous compute resources. These assumptions do not hold with dynamic, bandwidth-constrained P2P networks of consumer-grade devices.

2.2 Decentralized and Peer-to-Peer Inference

Recent work has begun to explore distributed inference over less reliable networks. Petals [1] demonstrated collaborative inference where users contribute GPU resources, but relies on central authority for peer discovery and assumes stable, high-bandwidth connections. Distributed-llama [14] takes an alternative approach using tensor parallelism over Ethernet to split models across consumer CPUs, but requires power-of-two node counts, supports only Llama-family architectures, and lacks P2P or NAT traversal capabilities. Exo [2] enables distributed inference by sharding models across a home cluster of consumer devices with memory-weighted partitioning, but is restricted to local networks, does not address NAT traversal, and supports only a limited set of model families. Lattica [20] provides cross-NAT communication for decentralized AI but operates as a networking layer without application-level inference protocols. Built upon Lattica, Parallax [15] provides a sovereign AI runtime for serving models across heterogeneous device pools using a two-phase scheduler (Table 1).

Table 1. Comparison of distributed on-device LLM inference systems. HyperCluster uniquely combines internet-scale P2P networking, selective loading, and broad model support. (Sel. Load = Selective Layer Loading, Wt. Tie = Weight-Tying Support)

System	Type	P2P	NAT	Sel. Load	Wt. Tie	Model Scope
Petals [1]	PP	✗	✗	✗	✗	Limited
Exo [2]	PP	✓	✗	✗	✗	Limited
Prima.cpp [9]	Ring-PP	✗	✗	✗	N/A	llama.cpp
Parallax [20]	PP	✓	✓	✓	✗	Broad (vLLM/SGLang)
distributed-llama	TP	✗	✗	✗	✗	Limited
HyperCluster	**Ring-PP**	✓	✓	✓	✓	**Broad (HF Models)**

2.3 Ring Topologies and Pipelined Inference

The ring all-reduce algorithm [11] is a well-established communication pattern for distributed computation. Beyond aggregation, ring topologies have recently been adopted as a compute-level communication pattern for LLM inference. TokenRing [17] uses bidirectional ring-based peer-to-peer transfers to overlap attention computation with inter-node communication for long-context inference. JARVIS [16] distributes LLM layers across edge nodes organized in a token ring over wireless links, where hidden states circulate through the ring for each generated token. However, both systems assume controlled local topologies and do not address internet-scale P2P connectivity or NAT traversal.

Prima.cpp [9] adapted a pipelined ring architecture for splitting LLMs across heterogeneous home devices, introducing pipelined-ring parallelism (PRP) to overlap disk I/O with computation and communication. However, Prima.cpp is built on llama.cpp, restricting it to GGUF-format models, and operates on static local clusters without P2P networking capabilities.

HyperCluster extends the ring pipeline concept by: (i) building on the Hugging Face Transformers ecosystem for broad model compatibility, (ii) implementing the protocol over Iroh's [10] P2P networking stack with QUIC-based direct transport for internet-scale operation, and (iii) introducing selective layer loading to dramatically reduce per-node memory requirements and model load times.

3   System Architecture

The HyperCluster architecture comprises four interconnected subsystems: a **Network Layer** for P2P communication, a **Partitioning Layer** for dynamic model sharding, an **Execution Layer** for ring-pipeline inference, and a **Loading Layer** for memory-efficient model materialization. Figure 1 provides an end-to-end overview.

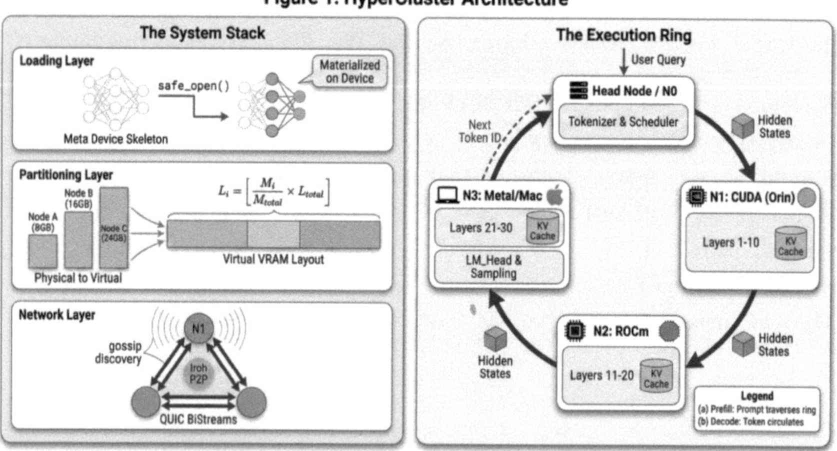

Fig. 1. HyperCluster system architecture. Nodes discover peers via Iroh's gossip protocol. They form a memory-ordered ring, selectively loading only their assigned layers, and then execute pipelined inference with QUIC-based tensor forwarding.

3.1   Network Layer: P2P Communication via Iroh and QUIC

HyperCluster builds its network layer upon **Iroh** [10], a content-addressed networking library providing primitives to build P2P networks like NAT traversal [3], gossip-based peer discovery, and document synchronization. Iroh utilizes QUIC [7] as its core transport protocol. Since QUIC is built on UDP and not TCP, and integrates TLS 1.3 by default, it provides encrypted, reliable communication with much lower handshake latency. Iroh leverages QUIC specifically for its robust connection migration and stream multiplexing features. These allow us to maintain stable P2P links in wireless networks where signal strength and IP addresses may fluctuate. Each node advertises its capabilities (available memory, compute class) through Iroh, and a `TopologyManager` maintains a real-time view of all active peers.

Direct Transport via QUIC: For tensor forwarding during inference, HyperCluster bypasses Iroh's document-based data exchange in favor of direct QUIC bidirectional streams (BiStreams). This provides several advantages over document-based transfer:

- **Low latency:** Direct stream-based RPC avoids the overhead of content-addressed blob storage and document synchronization.
- **Connection pooling:** Persistent `StreamHandle` objects maintain QUIC connections to ring neighbors, with multiplexed RPC calls over a single connection.
- **Binary frames:** Minimized encoding overhead compared to normal JSON-based protocols due to length-prefixed binary frames with msgpack serialization.

The wire format for tensor transmission consists of a 4-byte metadata length prefix, followed by JSON metadata (tensor shape, dtype, position IDs, attention mask), followed by raw tensor bytes. This format supports efficient numpy array reconstruction on the receiving end.

Pre-warmed Connections: Before inference begins, HyperCluster establishes QUIC connections to all ring neighbors via a pre-warming phase, sending lightweight ping/pong frames. This eliminates the 6–20 ms QUIC handshake latency that would otherwise be incurred on the first inference request.

3.2   Partitioning Layer: Memory-Weighted Sharding

To distribute a model with L layers across N heterogeneous nodes with memory capacities $M = \{m_1, m_2, \ldots, m_N\}$, HyperCluster employs a **memory-proportional partitioning strategy**. Nodes are sorted by available memory in descending order, establishing both the ring topology and the layer assignment. Each node i receives a number of layers proportional to its memory fraction of the total cluster memory. The partitioning algorithm is detailed in Algorithm 1.

For modern transformer architectures, layers have approximately uniform memory requirements, making layer count a reliable proxy for resource allocation. The resulting `LayerWindow` objects define contiguous layer ranges per node, which are used by both the loading layer and the execution layer.

Algorithm 1. Memory-Weighted Layer Partitioning

1: **Input:** Total layers L, Sorted nodes $\{N_1, \ldots, N_n\}$ with memories $\{m_1, \ldots, m_n\}$
2: **Output:** Layer assignments $W = \{w_1, \ldots, w_n\}$
3: $M_{\text{total}} \leftarrow \sum_{i=1}^{n} m_i$
4: $L_{\text{current}} \leftarrow 0$
5: **for** $i = 1$ **to** n **do**
6: $\quad f_i \leftarrow m_i / M_{\text{total}}$ {Memory fraction}
7: $\quad$ **if** $i = n$ **then**
8: $\quad\quad \ell_i \leftarrow L - L_{\text{current}}$ {Last node gets remaining}
9: $\quad$ **else**
10: $\quad\quad \ell_i \leftarrow \max(1, \lfloor f_i \times L \rfloor)$ {At least 1 layer}
11: $\quad$ **end if**
12: $\quad w_i \leftarrow \texttt{LayerWindow}(L_{\text{current}}, L_{\text{current}} + \ell_i - 1, L)$
13: $\quad L_{\text{current}} \leftarrow L_{\text{current}} + \ell_i$
14: **end for**
15: **return** W

3.3 Loading Layer: Selective Layer Loading from Safetensors

Traditional model loading via `from_pretrained()` loads *all* model weights into memory and then frees unneeded layers, a process that is both slow and memory-wasteful when a node requires only a subset of layers. HyperCluster introduces **selective layer loading**, which materializes only the tensors required by each node's assigned shard.

Loading Procedure. The selective loading process consists of five steps:

1. **Empty Skeleton Creation:** Using `init_empty_weights()`, create the full model architecture on a `meta` device. This allocates zero bytes, producing only the computational graph.
2. **Weight Key Filtering:** Determine which tensor keys are needed based on the assigned layer range. For a node assigned layers $[s, e]$ out of L total:
   - If $s = 0$ (first shard): include embedding weights (`embed_tokens`).
   - If $e = L - 1$ (last shard): include final layer norm and `lm_head` weights.
   - Always: include weights for layers s through e.
3. **File-to-Key Mapping:** Parse the safetensors index file to build a mapping from checkpoint files to the subset of needed keys in each file, minimizing I/O by opening only files containing relevant weights.
4. **Targeted Materialization:** Load required tensors via `safe_open()` and place them on the target device using `set_module_tensor_to_device()`. Unneeded layers remain on the `meta` device at zero cost.
5. **Weight-Tying Restoration:** For models with `tie_word_embeddings=True`, explicitly re-tie the language model head to the embedding weights.

3.4   Weight-Tying Preservation

Many modern SLMs (e.g., Llama-3.2 [4], Qwen3 [19]) use *weight tying*, where the language model head (`lm_head`) shares weights with the token embedding layer (`embed_tokens`). In standard `from_pretrained()` loading, this sharing is implicit: the framework recognizes the tie and avoids storing duplicate weights. However, selective loading via `init_empty_weights()` followed by per-tensor `set_module_tensor_to_device()` breaks this implicit tie, leaving `lm_head` on the meta device with uninitialized (all-zero) weights. This produces all-zero logits, leading to random token sampling and gibberish output.

HyperCluster addresses this with explicit weight-tying restoration after selective loading:

- **First-and-last shard** (single node holding both embeddings and lm_head): After loading, explicitly set `lm_head.weight = embed_tokens.weight`, re-establishing the tie.
- **Last-only shard** (node without embeddings but with lm_head): Load `embed_tokens.weight` from the safetensors file and assign it to `lm_head.weight`, even though the node does not use the embedding layer for forward computation.
- **Verification:** After restoration, verify that `lm_head.weight` resides on an actual device (not meta) and contains non-zero values.

3.5   Execution Layer: Ring-Pipeline Inference

Following layer assignment and selective loading, nodes form a deterministic logical ring $N_0 \rightarrow N_1 \rightarrow \cdots \rightarrow N_{n-1} \rightarrow N_0$, where rank corresponds to the memory-based ordering. Node N_0 (rank 0) holds the initial layers including token embeddings and serves as the entry point for inference requests.

Ring Position and Inference State. Each node maintains a `RingPosition` recording its rank, world size, and the identities of its predecessor and successor in the ring. The inference state flowing through the ring consists of:

- **Hidden states:** The intermediate activations ($\mathbb{R}^{1 \times d}$ for single-token generation), passed from node to node.
- **Position IDs:** Required for Rotary Position Embeddings (RoPE), incremented at each generation step.
- **Attention mask:** Grows with each generated token to maintain causal attention.
- **KV cache:** Each node maintains a local cache only for its assigned layers, ensuring that only the compact hidden states flow through the ring.

Pipeline Operation. Inference proceeds in two phases:

1. **Prefill Phase:** The initial prompt tokens are processed in a single forward pass through the ring. Each node executes its assigned layers sequentially, passing hidden states to its successor via the QUIC direct transport.

2. **Autoregressive Generation Phase:** For each new token, the single-token input traverses the entire ring. The final node (N_{n-1}) computes output logits, samples the next token using nucleus sampling with configurable temperature and top-p parameters, and the token is propagated back to the head node to begin the next generation step.

Cycle Calculation. If a model has more layers than can be covered in a single pass through the ring (i.e., the sum of all layer windows is less than the total layer count), multiple cycles through the ring are required. The number of cycles is computed as $k = \lceil L/\sum_i w_i \rceil$, where w_i is the layer count assigned to node i. In practice, with sufficient nodes, $k = 1$.

The complete autoregressive generation loop for a 3-node cluster is illustrated in Fig. 2.

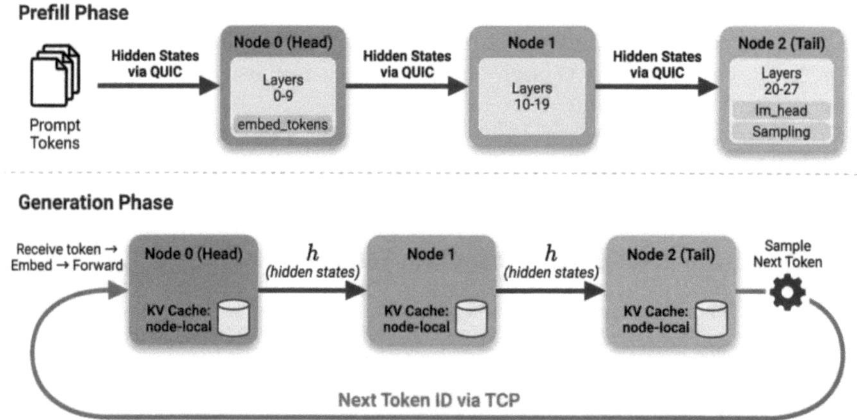

Fig. 2. Ring pipeline autoregressive generation across 3 nodes (28 layers). **Top:** In prefill phase prompt tokens traverse the ring once and each node processes its assigned layers and forwards hidden states via QUIC. **Bottom:** In generation phase, each new token cycles through all nodes; the final node samples the next token and feeds it back to the head node.

3.6   Transformer Layer Sharding via Dynamic Wrapping

The sharding engine implements runtime layer extraction through the wrapper class `TransformersShard`, which dynamically isolates assigned layers from any Hugging Face `AutoModelForCausalLM` instance. The wrapper categorizes shards by their role:

– **Initial Shard (N_0):** Executes token embedding (`embed_tokens`) followed by layers $[0, k_0]$.

- **Intermediate Shards** $(N_i,\ 0 < i < n - 1)$**:** Process layers $[k_{i-1} + 1, k_i]$ on received hidden states.
- **Final Shard** (N_{n-1})**:** Executes layers $[k_{n-2} + 1, L - 1]$, applies final layer normalization, and projects to vocabulary via the language model head.

Critical Implementation Details. Two implementation details are essential for correct distributed inference:

1. **Config Patching:** The model's `num_hidden_layers` configuration is over-ridden to match the shard's layer count. This is critical because the `DynamicCache` (used in transformers $\geq$ 5.2.0) pre-allocates cache storage based on this value; without patching, cache indices are misaligned, producing incorrect attention computations.
2. **Layer Re-indexing:** The `layer_idx` attribute on each attention module is re-indexed to $[0, |\text{shard}| - 1]$, ensuring that KV cache entries are stored at the correct indices within the node-local cache, regardless of the layer's position in the full model.

Distributed State Management. For correct autoregressive generation, each forward pass transmits hidden states along with position IDs and the attention mask. The KV cache is *not* transmitted between nodes; instead, each node maintains and updates a local cache only for its assigned layers. This design ensures that only the hidden states $(\mathbb{R}^{1 \times d})$ flow through the ring, while the much larger KV cache (scaling with sequence length and layer count) remains node-local.

4　Evaluation and Results

4.1　Experimental Setup

Hardware Configuration. Our testbed consists of three heterogeneous consumer devices, summarized in Table 2.

We evaluate on three models: Qwen3-0.6B [19] (28 layers, $d = 1024$), Llama-3.2-1B-Instruct [4] (16 layers, $d = 2048$), and Llama-3.2-3B-Instruct [4] (28 layers, $d = 3072$). All three use `tie_word_embeddings=True` to enable our weight-tying preservation mechanism. We report three primary metrics:

1. **Time to First Token (TTFT):** Latency from query submission to the first generated token
2. **Average Time Per Token (ATPT):** Mean latency per generated token during autoregressive generation
3. **Tokens per second:** Throughput

Table 2. Testbed device config. Nodes communicate over the Iroh P2P network across separate physical networks.

	Device 1 (D1)	Device 2 (D2)	Device 3 (D3)
Device	MacBook Air M2	Mac Mini	Linux Laptop
CPU	Apple M2	Apple Silicon	Intel i5
RAM	16 GB	8 GB	8 GB
GPU	Apple Silicon	Apple Silicon	None (CPU-only)

Table 3. Latency breakdown across cluster configurations. (All metrics are averaged across 32, 64, and 128 token generation sequences.)

Setup	TTFT (ms)	ATPT (ms)	Tokens/sec
1-Node			
Qwen3 0.6B	661	88.2	11.34
Llama 3.2 1B	942	130.3	7.68
Llama 3.2 3B	1,847	292.2	3.42
2-Node			
Qwen3 0.6B	4,023	247.6	4.04
Llama 3.2 1B	13,481	293.1	3.41
Llama 3.2 3B	21,321	438.2	2.28
3-Node			
Qwen3 0.6B	8,356	302.7	3.30
Llama 3.2 1B	9,866	406.4	2.46
Llama 3.2 3B	10,850	428.0	2.34

4.2   Inference Performance

Single-Node Baseline. On a single node (MacBook Air M2), Qwen3-0.6B achieves 11.34 tokens/sec with 661 ms TTFT, Llama-3.2-1B reaches 6.96 tokens/sec with 942 ms TTFT, and the larger Llama-3.2-3B produces 3.42 tokens/sec with 1,847 ms TTFT. These baselines establish the performance ceiling without communication overhead and confirm that per-token compute cost scales with model size.

Multi-node Scaling. Moving to 2 or 3 nodes introduces communication overhead dominated by QUIC tensor transfers over the P2P network. For Llama-3.2-1B, TTFT increases from 942 ms (1-node) to 13.48 s (2-node), but drops to 9.86 s (3-node) because distributing fewer layers speeds up the prefill phase. However, during generation, ATPT strictly increases from 130.3 ms (1-node) to 293.1 ms (2-node) and 406.4 ms (3-node). The reduction in per-node compute time is outweighed by the latency of an additional network hop, causing throughput to drop, from 3.41 tokens/sec (2-node) to 2.46 tokens/sec (3-node).

Table 3 presents the latency breakdown across 1, 2, and 3-node configurations. The larger Llama-3.2-3B demonstrates that HyperCluster can distribute models up to 3B parameters across consumer devices, achieving 1.72 tokens/sec on 2 nodes and 1.15 tokens/sec on 3 nodes. This model in float16 is around 6.5GB, which, including the OS overhead, is more than what 8GB RAM devices can handle. The decrease in throughput on the 3-node setup occurs because the model's larger hidden dimension ($d = 3072$) increases the volume of tensor data transferred per hop, making communication overhead more pronounced (Table 4).

Table 4. Network performance breakdown per generation step. Transfer size reflects the hidden state tensor ($\mathbb{R}^{1 \times d}$, float32) transmitted per ring hop.

Model	Nodes	Net Wait (ms)	Transfer Size (KB)
Qwen3-0.6B	2	168.3	4.0
Qwen3-0.6B	3	273.4	4.0
Llama 3.2 1B	2	183.5	8.0
Llama 3.2 1B	3	172.9	8.0
Llama 3.2 3B	2	194.0	12.0
Llama 3.2 3B	3	576.3	12.0

Table 5. Per-token timing breakdown for 2-node inference, decomposing ATPT into compute vs. communication components.

Component	Qwen3-0.6B		Llama 3.2 1B		Llama 3.2 3B	
	ms	%	ms	%	ms	%
Inference (compute)	79.3	32.0	109.6	37.4	244.2	55.7
Network wait	168.3	68.0	183.5	62.6	194.0	44.3
Total ATPT	**247.6**	**100**	**293.1**	**100**	**438.2**	**100**

5 Discussion

5.1 Communication Bottleneck Analysis

Our results reveal that the primary bottleneck in multi-node inference is communication latency, not computation. Table 5 shows that network wait accounts for 68% of per-token time for Qwen3-0.6B (2-node) but only 44% for Llama-3.2-3B, where the larger model's compute cost begins to dominate. Hence, communication optimization will yield the greatest benefit for smaller models, while larger models amortize network overhead through increased per-node computation (Table 6).

Table 6. Model loading time and peak memory comparison: full loading (`from_pretrained`) vs. selective loading across all evaluated models.

Model	Shard Type	Layers	Load Time (s)	Speedup
Qwen3-0.6B	Full load	0–27	1.52	1.0×
	HEAD (0–17)	18/28	0.36	4.2×
	WORKER (18–27)	10/28	0.32	4.8×
Llama-3.2-1B	Full load	0–15	3.87	1.0×
	HEAD (0–9)	10/16	1.12	3.5×
	WORKER (10–15)	6/16	0.74	5.2×
Llama-3.2-3B	Full load	0–27	11.43	1.0×
	HEAD (0–17)	18/28	4.21	2.7×
	WORKER (18–27)	10/28	2.58	4.4×

1. **Per-token ring traversal:** Each generated token requires hidden states to traverse the full ring, incurring QUIC transfer latency at each hop. With P2P connections spanning separate networks, round-trip times of 20–100 ms per hop dominate the per-token cost for smaller models.
2. **Hidden dimension scaling:** Transfer size scales linearly with hidden dimension: 4 KB for Qwen3 ($d = 1024$), 8 KB for Llama-1B ($d = 2048$), and 12 KB for Llama-3B ($d = 3072$). This directly impacts network wait time, particularly for 3-node configurations where each token traverses two inter-node hops.

5.2   Limitations and Future Work

1. **Communication optimization:** Network latency dominates multi-node performance. Future work will explore tensor compression, quantized activation transfer, and speculative prefetching to reduce per-hop transfer costs.
2. **Heterogeneity-aware scheduling:** The current memory-proportional partitioning does not account for compute heterogeneity. Adopting approaches like Halda [9] that co-optimize compute, memory, and communication would improve performance on diverse hardware.
3. **Fault tolerance:** The system currently requires inference restart on node failure. Implementing checkpoint-based recovery and dynamic ring reconfiguration would improve robustness.
4. **Model quantization:** Integrating quantization (e.g., GPTQ, AWQ, GGUF) would reduce both memory footprint and tensor transfer sizes, enabling larger models and faster communication.
5. **Broader architecture support:** Extending to vision-language models, Mixture-of-Experts (MoE) architectures, and speculative decoding would broaden applicability (Fig. 3 and 4).

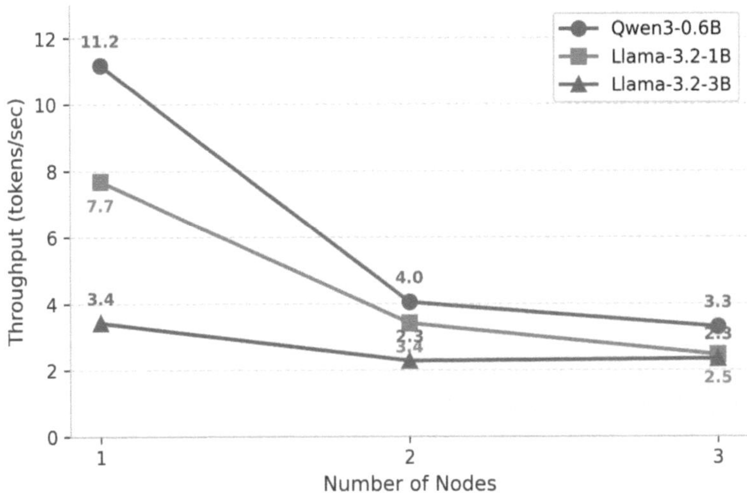

Fig. 3. Throughput (tokens/sec) scaling across cluster configurations. Single-node throughput degrades with added nodes due to communication overhead, though Llama-3.2-1B shows improved 3-node throughput from reduced per-node compute.

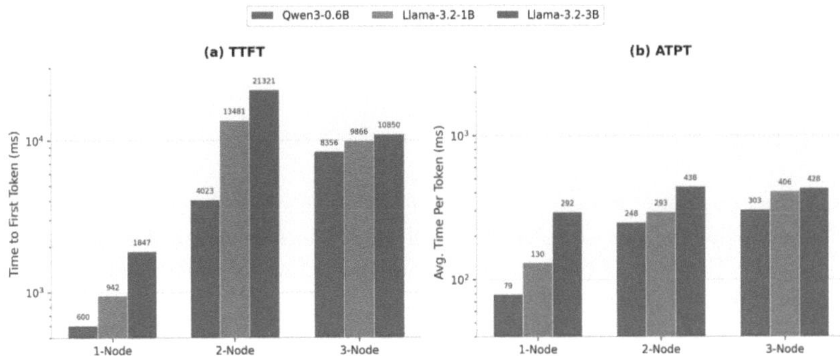

Fig. 4. Latency comparison across cluster configurations. Communication overhead dominates multi-node setups, with Qwen3-0.6B showing more favorable scaling due to its smaller hidden dimension.

6   Conclusion

We present HyperCluster, a decentralized system for large language model inference across heterogeneous wireless networks. By combining P2P networking via Iroh with QUIC-based direct transport, memory-weighted sharding, selective layer loading from safetensors, weight-tying preservation, and ring-based pipelined execution, HyperCluster demonstrates that collaborative AI inference is practical on resource-constrained consumer devices without centralized coordination.

Our key contributions include:

- A fully decentralized ring-pipeline protocol with pre-warmed QUIC connections for low-latency tensor forwarding
- Selective layer loading that achieves up to 5.2× faster load times compared to full model loading
- A weight-tying mechanism that ensures correct inference for models with shared embedding weights
- A generalizable sharding engine compatible with any Hugging Face model.

Our evaluation on heterogeneous consumer devices with models up to 3B parameters validates the architecture and identifies communication latency as the primary scaling bottleneck, providing clear direction for future optimization.

HyperCluster opens new possibilities for privacy-preserving, AI-native wireless applications, reducing dependence on cloud infrastructure while enabling collaborative intelligence at the edge.

Acknowledgments. This work builds upon ideas from the Exo project for model sharding, Prima.cpp for ring pipeline architectures, and Iroh for P2P networking primitives. We thank the open-source community for these foundational contributions.

Disclosure of Interests. The authors have no competing interests to declare that are relevant to the content of this article.

References

1. Borzunov, A., et al.: Petals: collaborative inference and fine-tuning of large models. In: Proceedings of the 61st Annual Meeting of the Association for Computational Linguistics (Volume 3: System Demonstrations), pp. 558–568 (2023). https://doi.org/10.18653/v1/2023.acl-demo.54
2. ExoLabs: EXO: run your own ai cluster at home with everyday devices (2024). https://github.com/exo-explore/exo
3. Ford, B., Srisuresh, P., Kegel, D.: Peer-to-peer communication across network address translators. In: Proceedings of the 2005 USENIX Annual Technical Conference (USENIX ATC 2005), p. 13 (2005)
4. Grattafiori, A., et al.: The LLaMA 3 herd of models. arXiv preprint arXiv:2407.21783 (2024)
5. HuggingFace: Safetensors: a simple, safe way to store and distribute tensors (2022). https://github.com/huggingface/safetensors
6. HyperSpace: Hyperspace: Peer-to-peer AI network (2024). https://hyperspace.computer/bittorrent-for-ai.pdf
7. Iyengar, J., Thomson, M.: QUIC: a UDP-based multiplexed and secure transport. RFC 9000, IETF (2021). https://doi.org/10.17487/RFC9000
8. Jaghouar, S., et al.: Intellect-1 technical report. arXiv preprint arXiv:2412.01152 (2024)
9. Li, Z., et al.: Prima.cpp: Fast 30-70b LLM inference on heterogeneous and low-resource home clusters. arXiv preprint arXiv:2504.08791 (2025)
10. n0, Inc.: Iroh: P2P for everyone (2024). https://www.iroh.computer

11. Patarasuk, P., Yuan, X.: Bandwidth-optimal all-reduce algorithms for clusters of workstations. J. Parallel Distrib. Comput. **69**(2), 117–124 (2009). https://doi.org/10.1016/j.jpdc.2008.09.002
12. Rasley, J., Rajbhandari, S., Ruwase, O., He, Y.: DeepSpeed: system optimizations enable training deep learning models with over 100 billion parameters. In: Proceedings of the 26th ACM SIGKDD International Conference on Knowledge Discovery & Data Mining, pp. 3505–3506 (2020). https://doi.org/10.1145/3394486.3406703
13. Shoeybi, M., et al.: Megatron-LM: training multi-billion parameter language models using model parallelism (2019)
14. Tadych, B.: Distributed-LLaMA: connect home devices into a powerful cluster to accelerate LLM inference (2024). https://github.com/b4rtaz/distributed-llama
15. Tong, C., et al.: Parallax: efficient LLM inference service over decentralized environment (2025)
16. Tong, J., et al.: JARVIS: disjoint large language models on radio VLANs for inference serving (2024)
17. Wang, Z., et al.: Tokenring: an efficient parallelism framework for infinite-context LLMs via bidirectional communication (2024)
18. Wolf, T., et al.: Transformers: state-of-the-art natural language processing. In: Proceedings of the 2020 Conference on Empirical Methods in Natural Language Processing: System Demonstrations, pp. 38–45 (2020). https://doi.org/10.18653/v1/2020.emnlp-demos.6
19. Yang, A., et al.: Qwen3 technical report (2025)
20. Yang, W., et al.: Lattica: a decentralized cross-NAT communication framework for scalable ai inference and training. arXiv preprint arXiv:2510.00183 (2025)
21. Zheng, L., et al.: Alpa: automating inter-and {Intra-Operator} parallelism for distributed deep learning. In: 16th USENIX Symposium on Operating Systems Design and Implementation (OSDI 2022), pp. 559–578 (2022)

Improving Federated Graph Recommendation with Semantic Guidance

Thi Minh Chau Nguyen[1]([✉]), Hien Trang Nguyen[2], Duc Anh Nguyen[3],
Van Ho-Long[4,5], Thanh Trung Huynh[6], and Zhao Ren[7]

[1] Foreign Trade University, Hanoi, Vietnam
ntminhchau97@gmail.com
[2] Griffith University, Brisbane, Australia
[3] Hanoi University of Science and Technology, Hanoi, Vietnam
[4] International University, Ho Chi Minh City, Ho Chi Minh City, Vietnam
[5] Vietnam National University, Ho Chi Minh City, Ho Chi Minh City, Vietnam
[6] VinUniversity, Hanoi, Vietnam
[7] University of Bremen, Bremen, Germany

Abstract. Graph-based recommendation models effectively capture high-order collaborative signals from user–item interaction graphs. Federated learning (FL) enables privacy-preserving training across distributed clients. However, directly aggregating graph representations under FL is challenging: locally learned structural embeddings are not globally aligned under non-IID data distributions, and naive parameter averaging fails to recover cross-client relational structure. Existing federated graph-based approaches primarily rely on structural aggregation, yet overlook the global semantic knowledge encoded in large language models (LLMs). In this work, we propose a semantic–structural federated graph recommendation framework that leverages LLM embeddings to guide cross-client alignment. Each client learns user representations from its local interaction graph and summarizes typical interaction patterns into compact semantic vectors using a frozen LLM encoder. These vectors are sent to the server, which identifies semantically related patterns across different clients and combines their structural representations accordingly. The updated representations are then returned to clients to refine subsequent local training. This design enables collaboration guided by shared semantic understanding without exposing raw interaction data, preserving both recommendation accuracy and privacy. Experiments on benchmark datasets demonstrate consistent improvements over existing federated graph-based baselines.

Keywords: Federated learning · Graph-based recommendation · Large language models · Semantic alignment · Privacy-preserving learning

1 Introduction

Personalized recommendation systems have become a core component of modern online services, including e-commerce, media streaming, and social platforms.

© IFIP International Federation for Information Processing 2026
Published by Springer Nature Switzerland AG 2026
A. Nunes Alonso and R. Palmieri (Eds.): DAIS 2026, LNCS 16591, pp. 36–52, 2026.
https://doi.org/10.1007/978-3-032-27358-1_3

Classical collaborative filtering techniques [7,8] learn latent user and item representations from large-scale interaction data stored in centralized servers. More recently, graph neural networks (GNNs) have demonstrated strong capability in modeling high-order user–item relationships by propagating information over interaction graphs, as exemplified by LightGCN [6]. Despite their effectiveness, these centralized paradigms require collecting and storing raw user interaction logs, raising substantial privacy and regulatory concerns.

Federated learning (FL) offers a natural alternative by enabling collaborative model training without sharing raw data. In federated recommender systems, each client (e.g., user device or organization) retains its local interaction history and contributes model updates to a central server [1]. Subsequent work has improved federated recommendation from multiple perspectives, including handling heterogeneous client distributions [33] FedRecon [21] and PFedRec [38] further adapt global models to client-specific preferences. However, most federated methods rely on parameter aggregation schemes that implicitly assume structural compatibility across clients.

Graph-based federated recommendation has emerged to better exploit relational structures under privacy constraints. Approaches such as FedPerGNN [26], GPFedRec [39], UFGraphFR [25], and GFed-PP [16] incorporate graph modeling or user-relation construction into federated optimization. These methods demonstrate that structural signals beyond independent user modeling can improve personalization. Nevertheless, they typically align models at the embedding or user-graph level, assuming that structurally similar patterns across clients are directly comparable. In realistic federated environments, client data are highly non-IID: user communities on different devices may share semantic preferences but exhibit divergent local graph structures. Direct structural averaging or graph aggregation may therefore fail to capture cross-client semantic consistency.

In parallel, large language models (LLMs) have shown remarkable ability to encode rich semantic information from textual descriptions and behavioral contexts [13,24,27]. LLM-based recommendation frameworks demonstrate that semantic abstraction can complement ID-based collaborative signals, particularly when interaction data are sparse or heterogeneous. In federated settings, recent efforts such as GPT-FedRec [37] and FELLAS [35] leverage LLMs to enhance representation learning or sequential modeling under privacy constraints. However, existing approaches primarily leverage LLMs to refine local representations or enrich item semantics, rather than employing them to guide structural alignment across distributed clients in federated environments.

These observations motivate a central question: *can semantic abstraction be used to regulate structural collaboration in federated graph recommendation?* Instead of aggregating graph embeddings directly, we argue that cross-client alignment should first be established at the semantic level, and then modulate structural merging accordingly. Semantic similarity provides a more stable signal under heterogeneous distributions, as communities that share preference intent may not exhibit identical graph topology. By prioritizing semantic alignment and using structural similarity as a secondary modulation, federated collaboration can become both more robust and more interpretable.

In this work, we propose SemFGRec (*Semantic Federated Graph Recommendation*), a semantic-guided federated graph learning framework designed for non-IID environments. SemFGRec operates by learning collaborative representations from local interaction graphs using a lightweight graph encoder [6], abstracting preference patterns into higher-level descriptors, and enabling semantically consistent knowledge sharing across clients without exposing raw interaction data. Instead of blindly aggregating structural parameters, SemFGRec introduces a semantic-aware collaboration mechanism that selectively regularizes structurally compatible representations across clients. This design preserves personalization while enabling principled cross-client knowledge transfer.

In summary, our contributions are threefold:

- We introduce SemFGRec, a semantic-guided framework for federated graph recommendation that uses semantic signals to regulate how structural patterns are shared across clients.
- We design a semantic-aware collaboration mechanism improving robustness under non-IID client distributions without transmitting raw interaction data.
- We conduct comprehensive experiments against strong centralized, federated, and graph-based baselines, demonstrating consistent gains and improved stability across heterogeneous environments.

2   Related Works

Federated Recommender Systems. Federated recommendation has emerged to reconcile personalization with strict data protection requirements [12,32]. Subsequent research improved optimization under heterogeneous client distributions [33], strengthened privacy guarantees through differential privacy and secure aggregation [11,20,34] PFedRec [38] introduces dual personalization mechanisms for both users and items. Meta-learning and lightweight parameter adaptation have also been explored to improve scalability. Extensions include decentralized aggregation without a single central server (DeFedGCN) [4], and privacy-preserving knowledge-graph-aware recommendation frameworks such as FedKGRec [14]. Cross-domain federated graph transfer is studied in FedGCDR [29]. Explainable and knowledge-graph-enhanced federated frameworks further improve transparency and interpretability [9,22]. Despite these advances, existing methods primarily emphasize collaborative optimization, privacy mechanisms, or personalization, without explicitly incorporating semantic abstraction for cross-client structural alignment.

Federated Recommender Systems with LLM. Large language models (LLMs) have recently been integrated into recommender systems to enhance representation learning and generative capability [13,27]. Some studies employ LLMs as domain-agnostic recommenders [24], while others combine retrieval-augmented generation with federated learning (e.g., GPT-FedRec [37]). Federated LLM-based recommendation frameworks include FELLRec [40] and FEL-LAS [35]. Broader perspectives on federated LLM training are discussed in recent surveys and benchmarks [30,31]. In centralized settings, multi-behavior graph modeling such as MBH-GNN [23] demonstrates that behavior-aware semantic embeddings can improve recommendation accuracy. However, most LLM-based federated approaches focus on representation enhancement or re-ranking, rather than using semantic abstractions to regulate structural collaboration across distributed clients in federated environments.

Federated Recommender Systems with Graph. Graph neural networks (GNNs) have become a dominant paradigm for recommendation due to their ability to capture high-order user–item interactions. LightGCN [6] simplifies graph convolution to linear neighborhood aggregation and serves as an effective backbone for collaborative filtering. In federated environments, FeSoG [10] extends graph modeling to social recommendation under privacy constraints. FedPerGNN [26] enables decentralized graph learning with privacy-preserving graph expansion. GPFedRec [39] constructs user-relation graphs from personalized item embeddings to guide aggregation. UFGraphFR [25] incorporates semantic similarity to build federated user graphs. GFed-PP [16] leverages both private and public user data for privacy-aware aggregation. Subgraph-level privacy-preserving learning is explored in PFGRS [19]. Vertical federated graph training is studied in VerFedGNN [15]. Additional enhancements integrate structured clustering and graph attention within federated learning frameworks [28]. Although these approaches combine graph modeling with federated optimization, they operate primarily at the embedding or user-graph level and do not perform semantic-guided community-level structural merging.

Overall, prior research addresses collaborative optimization, graph modeling, personalization, knowledge graphs, and LLM-based enhancement largely in isolation. In contrast, our framework integrates semantic abstraction and structural graph modeling at the community level, enabling semantic-first alignment to improve robustness under heterogeneous federated environments.

3   Problem Formulation

We consider a federated graph-based recommendation setting with K clients and a central server. Each client $k \in \{1, \ldots, K\}$ holds a local user–item interaction graph

$$\mathcal{G}_k = (\mathcal{U}_k, \mathcal{I}_k, \mathcal{E}_k),$$

where $\mathcal{U}_k$ denotes the set of local users, $\mathcal{I}_k \subseteq \mathcal{I}$ denotes the items observed by client k, and $\mathcal{E}_k \subseteq \mathcal{U}_k \times \mathcal{I}_k$ represents observed interactions (e.g., clicks, purchases, or ratings).

The global item set is denoted by $\mathcal{I}$ with $|\mathcal{I}| = M$. Users are disjoint across clients, i.e., $\mathcal{U}_k \cap \mathcal{U}_{k'} = \emptyset$ for $k \neq k'$, while items may be shared. Raw interaction data $\mathcal{E}_k$ and user identities are kept on-device and are not transmitted to the server, reducing direct exposure of user behavior.

3.1   Federated Objective

The goal is to learn client-specific user embeddings $\{h_u \in \mathbb{R}^d \mid u \in \mathcal{U}_k\}$ for each client k and a shared global item embedding matrix $E_I \in \mathbb{R}^{M \times d}$ such that recommendation quality is maximized while preserving data locality.

For each client k, we adopt the Bayesian Personalized Ranking (BPR) objective as the local optimization target:

$$\mathcal{L}_{\text{rank}}^k = -\mathbb{E}_{(u,i^+,i^-) \sim \mathcal{D}_k} \log \sigma(\langle h_u, h_{i+} \rangle - \langle h_u, h_{i-} \rangle), \tag{1}$$

where $\mathcal{D}_k$ denotes the local training distribution constructed from $\mathcal{E}_k$. Here, (u, i^+, i^-) represents a user, a positive item, and a negative item, respectively.

In a standard federated learning framework, the global objective can be written as:

$$\min_{\{h_u\}, E_I} \sum_{k=1}^{K} \mathcal{L}_{\text{rank}}^k, \tag{2}$$

subject to the constraint that raw interaction data remain local.

3.2   Challenges Under Non-IID Graph Distributions

In practice, client data distributions are non-IID. Different clients may exhibit distinct preference domains, interaction densities, and item popularity patterns. Under such heterogeneity, naive federated averaging of model parameters does not guarantee alignment of learned representations.

In particular, user embeddings are client-specific and cannot be aggregated directly. Even for shared item embeddings, simple averaging may mix incompatible preference signals across clients. Moreover, graph structures learned locally may encode structurally similar patterns that correspond to semantically different user intents.

3.3   Semantic–Structural Alignment Objective

To address these challenges, we introduce community-level representations on each client. Let $\{\mathcal{U}_{k,c}\}_{c=1}^{C_k}$ denote preference communities identified on client k. For each community, we compute:

- a structural prototype $P_{k,c} \in \mathbb{R}^d$, summarizing collaborative preference geometry, and
- a semantic embedding $S_{k,c} \in \mathbb{R}^d$, summarizing thematic characteristics derived from item content.

Our objective extends the standard federated ranking loss by introducing a cross-client alignment term:

$$\mathcal{L}_k = \mathcal{L}_{\text{rank}}^k + \lambda_{\text{align}} \sum_{c=1}^{C_k} \left\| P_{k,c} - \tilde{P}_g^{(t)} \right\|_2^2, \tag{3}$$

where $\tilde{P}_g^{(t)}$ denotes the merged structural prototype of semantically aligned communities across clients.

The key idea is to perform structural collaboration only when semantic consistency exists. By aligning community prototypes rather than individual user embeddings, we enable knowledge transfer across clients while maintaining personalization and privacy.

In summary, the problem is to design a federated optimization procedure that:

- learns collaborative representations from local interaction graphs,
- identifies semantically coherent preference communities,
- merges structurally compatible communities across clients, and
- improves recommendation accuracy without sharing raw interaction data.

4 Methodology

Figure 1 illustrates the overall pipeline of `SemFGRec`. At each communication round, clients first learn user and item representations from their local interaction graphs using a lightweight GNN encoder. Based on the learned user embeddings, each client extracts preference communities and derives two complementary descriptors: a structural prototype $P_{k,c}$ summarizing collaborative patterns and a semantic embedding $S_{k,c}$ obtained by encoding the summarized metadata of representative items. The server then performs row-wise item aggregation and constructs a semantic-first community graph across clients, where structural similarity modulates semantic alignment. Communities that satisfy the merging criterion are grouped and averaged to form global prototypes, which are broadcast back to clients for alignment-aware optimization. This iterative procedure enables cross-client semantic consistency while preserving local personalization under federated constraints.

4.1 Local Collaborative Representation Learning

On each client, we learn user and item representations from the local user–item interaction graph using a LightGCN-style encoder [6]. Given the normalized adjacency matrix $\tilde{A}_k$, embeddings are propagated for L_g layers:

$$H_k^{(l+1)} = \tilde{A}_k H_k^{(l)}. \tag{4}$$

The final embedding of user u and item i is obtained by aggregating representations from all layers:

$$h_u = \sum_{l=0}^{L_g} \alpha_l h_u^{(l)}, \qquad h_i = \sum_{l=0}^{L_g} \alpha_l h_i^{(l)}, \tag{5}$$

where $\alpha_l = \frac{1}{L_g+1}$ in our implementation. This encoder captures high-order collaborative signals through neighborhood propagation while keeping the architecture simple. A lightweight design is preferable in federated settings because

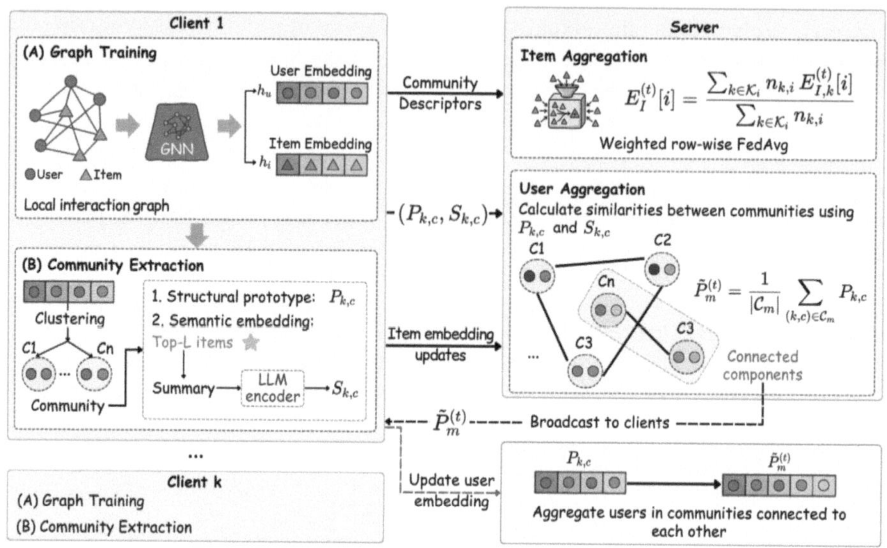

Fig. 1. Overall framework of `SemFGRec`. Each client performs local graph-based representation learning and adaptive community abstraction, producing structural prototypes $P_{k,c}$ and semantic descriptors $S_{k,c}$. The server aggregates item embeddings and constructs a semantic-guided community graph to merge aligned communities, generating global prototypes that are broadcast back for alignment-aware local refinement.

it reduces training variance across clients and makes the contribution of the semantic–structural merging mechanism easier to isolate.

Each client first minimizes the local ranking objective $\mathcal{L}^k_{\text{rank}}$ defined in Sect. 3:

$$\mathcal{L}^k_{\text{rank}} = -\mathbb{E}_{(u,i^+,i^-)\sim\mathcal{D}_k} \log \sigma(\langle h_u, h_{i^+}\rangle - \langle h_u, h_{i^-}\rangle),\qquad(6)$$

which encourages observed interactions to receive higher scores than sampled negatives.

4.2   Adaptive Community Abstraction

After learning user embeddings $\{h_u\}$, each client partitions users into preference communities using HDBSCAN [2], a density-based clustering algorithm:

$$\{\mathcal{U}_{k,c}\}_{c=1}^{C_k} = \texttt{HDBSCAN}(\{h_u\}).\qquad(7)$$

HDBSCAN determines the number of clusters automatically based on embedding density. This is important in federated environments, where different clients may exhibit different levels of interaction sparsity and preference diversity. Fixing the number of communities would impose an artificial structural assumption that may not reflect local data characteristics.

For each community c, we compute a structural prototype:

$$P_{k,c} = \frac{1}{|\mathcal{U}_{k,c}|} \sum_{u \in \mathcal{U}_{k,c}} h_u. \tag{8}$$

This prototype summarizes the collaborative preference pattern of the community in embedding space.

To obtain a semantic abstraction, we first select the top-L items with the highest interaction frequency among users in $\mathcal{U}_{k,c}$. We then aggregate their textual metadata (e.g., titles and descriptions) to construct a community-level summary $x_{k,c}$, which is encoded using a frozen large language model:

$$S_{k,c} = \text{LLMEnc}(x_{k,c}). \tag{9}$$

The structural prototype $P_{k,c}$ captures interaction-driven similarity, whereas the semantic embedding $S_{k,c}$ captures thematic similarity derived from item content. These two representations provide complementary views of the same community.

4.3   Semantic-Guided Structural Merging

The server first aggregates item embeddings via row-wise weighted averaging:

$$E_I^{(t)}[i] = \frac{\sum_k n_{k,i} E_{I,k}[i]}{\sum_k n_{k,i}}. \tag{10}$$

To align communities across clients, we compute semantic similarity using cosine similarity:

$$s_{a,b} = \frac{S_a^\top S_b}{\|S_a\|\|S_b\|}. \tag{11}$$

Cosine similarity is appropriate because both LLM embeddings and collaborative embeddings encode information primarily in their direction rather than magnitude.

Structural similarity is computed similarly:

$$r_{a,b} = \frac{P_a^\top P_b}{\|P_a\|\|P_b\|}. \tag{12}$$

We combine the two similarities as:

$$q_{a,b} = s_{a,b} \left(1 + \lambda r_{a,b}\right). \tag{13}$$

In this formulation, semantic similarity acts as the primary alignment signal. Structural similarity only adjusts the strength of merging. This design prevents merging communities that exhibit similar interaction statistics but correspond to different semantic meanings. In other words, semantic coherence is required before structural compatibility is considered.

Communities are merged when $q_{a,b} > \delta$, and merged structural prototypes are computed as:

$$\tilde{P}_g^{(t)} = \frac{1}{|\mathcal{C}_g|} \sum_{a \in \mathcal{C}_g} P_a. \tag{14}$$

4.4   Alignment-Aware End-to-End Training

After receiving merged prototypes, each client optimizes the following alignment-aware objective:

$$\mathcal{L}_k = \mathcal{L}_{\text{rank}}^k + \lambda_{\text{align}} \sum_{c=1}^{C_k} \left\| P_{k,c} - \tilde{P}_g^{(t)} \right\|_2^2. \tag{15}$$

The first term preserves personalized ranking performance. The second term encourages structurally similar communities to remain aligned across clients when semantic consistency exists. We use a soft alignment term rather than directly replacing local prototypes. Hard replacement may override locally meaningful preference patterns, especially under non-IID conditions. The alignment loss encourages consistency with semantically aligned communities while preserving local personalization.

Across communication rounds, we jointly optimize collaborative representation learning and semantic-guided merging. This end-to-end process integrates structural interaction modeling with global semantic alignment, enabling effective federated recommendation while keeping raw interaction data local, and reducing direct exposure of user behavior.

4.5   Training Procedure

The overall procedure consists of two coordinated components executed at each communication round: (i) client-side structural learning with adaptive community abstraction, and (ii) server-side semantic-guided structural merging. Unlike fixed-cluster approaches, the number of communities is automatically determined per client, enabling adaptation to heterogeneous non-IID preference distributions.

Client-Side Procedure. Each client k performs collaborative representation learning using a lightweight bipartite graph encoder, followed by adaptive community detection in embedding space and semantic abstraction. The detailed procedure is described in Algorithm 1.

Server-Side Procedure. The server performs row-wise item aggregation and constructs a semantic-first community graph across all clients. Structural similarity modulates semantic alignment to prevent incompatible merges. Since each client uploads only sparse item updates and a compact set of community descriptors rather than raw interaction logs, the communication cost is bounded by the

---

Algorithm 1. Client-Side Procedure at Round t

Require: Global item embeddings $E_I^{(t-1)}$, local interaction graph $\mathcal{G}_k$, local epochs T_{local}, alignment epochs T_{align}, top-L representative items, alignment weight λ_{align}

1: Initialize local item embeddings $E_{I,k} \leftarrow E_I^{(t-1)}$
2: **(A) Collaborative structural learning (LightGCN-style)**
3: **for** $e = 1$ to T_{local} **do**
4:     Obtain user/item embeddings $\{h_u\}, \{h_i\}$ via a LightGCN-style encoder on $\mathcal{G}_k$
5:     Update local parameters by minimizing the BPR ranking loss $\mathcal{L}_{\text{rank}}$
6: **end for**
7: **(B) Adaptive community detection and semantic descriptors**
8: Cluster user embeddings $\{h_u\}$ via density-based clustering to obtain communities $\{\mathcal{U}_{k,c}\}_{c=1}^{C_k}$, where C_k is automatically determined
9: **for** each community $c \in \{1, \ldots, C_k\}$ **do**
10:     Compute structural prototype $P_{k,c} \leftarrow \frac{1}{|\mathcal{U}_{k,c}|} \sum_{u \in \mathcal{U}_{k,c}} h_u$
11:     Select representative items $I_{k,c}^{\text{top}} \leftarrow \texttt{TopItems}(\mathcal{U}_{k,c}, L)$ and summarize $x_{k,c} \leftarrow$ $\texttt{SummarizeItems}(I_{k,c}^{\text{top}})$
12:     Compute semantic embedding $S_{k,c} \leftarrow \texttt{LLMEnc}(x_{k,c})$
13: **end for**
14: Upload sparse item updates and community descriptors $\{(S_{k,c}, P_{k,c})\}_{c=1}^{C_k}$
15: **(C) Post-merge structural alignment**
16: **for** $e = 1$ to T_{align} **do**
17:     Recompute prototypes $\{P_{k,c}\}$ and retrieve the merged prototype $\tilde{P}_g^{(t)}$ for each local community
18:     Minimize $\mathcal{L}_k = \mathcal{L}_{\text{rank}} + \lambda_{\text{align}} \sum_{c=1}^{C_k} \left\| P_{k,c} - \tilde{P}_g^{(t)} \right\|_2^2$
19: **end for**

---

number of updated items and discovered communities on that client. On the server side, the additional processing scales with the number of received community descriptors, making the procedure practical for federated deployment. The detailed procedure is described in Algorithm 2.

5   Experiments

We conduct extensive experiments to evaluate the effectiveness and robustness of the proposed semantic–structural federated graph recommendation framework. Specifically, we aim to answer the following research questions:

- **RQ1:** Does the proposed method outperform strong centralized and federated recommendation baselines?
- **RQ2:** Is the proposed semantic–structural merging robust under varying degrees of non-IID data heterogeneity?
- **RQ3:** What is the contribution of each component in the framework?
- **RQ4:** Is the proposed method stable with respect to key hyperparameters?

Algorithm 2. Server-Side Procedure at Round t

Require: Client uploads $\{\Delta E_{I,k}\}$ and $\{(S_{k,c}, P_{k,c})\}$, modulation weight λ, threshold δ, top-K_{nn} neighbors

1: **(A) Row-wise item aggregation**
2: **for** each updated item i **do**
3:     Update $E_I^{(t)}[i] \leftarrow \frac{\sum_k n_{k,i} E_{I,k}[i]}{\sum_k n_{k,i}}$
4: **end for**
5: **(B) Semantic-guided community graph construction**
6: Let $\mathcal{V} = \{(k,c)\}$ denote all received communities
7: **for** candidate pairs (a,b) from top-K_{nn} semantic neighbors **do**
8:     Compute semantic similarity $s_{a,b} \leftarrow \frac{S_a^\top S_b}{\|S_a\|\|S_b\|}$
9:     Compute structural similarity $r_{a,b} \leftarrow \frac{P_a^\top P_b}{\|P_a\|\|P_b\|}$
10:    Compute combined similarity $q_{a,b} \leftarrow s_{a,b}(1 + \lambda r_{a,b})$
11:    Add edge (a,b) if $q_{a,b} > \delta$
12: **end for**
13: Identify connected components $\{\mathcal{C}_g\}_{g=1}^{G_t}$
14: **(C) Prototype merging**
15: **for** each component $\mathcal{C}_g$ **do**
16:    Compute merged prototype $\tilde{P}_g^{(t)} \leftarrow \frac{1}{|\mathcal{C}_g|} \sum_{a \in \mathcal{C}_g} P_a$
17: **end for**
18: Broadcast updated item embeddings $\{E_I^{(t)}\}$ and merged prototypes $\{\tilde{P}_g^{(t)}\}$

5.1 Experimental Setup

Datasets. We evaluate on three benchmark datasets: MovieLens-100K and MovieLens-1M [5], as well as Amazon Video [17]. MovieLens-100K contains 100,000 ratings from 943 users on 1,682 movies, while MovieLens-1M includes one million ratings from 6,040 users on 3,952 movies. Amazon Video provides user interactions together with textual metadata such as item titles and descriptions, and is considerably sparser than MovieLens. For all datasets, ratings are converted to implicit feedback, and users or items with fewer than five interactions are removed.

Evaluation Protocol. We adopt a leave-one-out evaluation protocol in which the most recent interaction of each user is held out for testing. For each test user, we rank the ground-truth item among 100 sampled negative items. Performance is measured using Hit Ratio at rank 10 (HR@10) and Normalized Discounted Cumulative Gain at rank 10 (NDCG@10) [23]. HR@10 measures whether the ground-truth item appears in the top-10 list, while NDCG@10 further considers ranking positions. All results are reported in percentage (%). To simulate federated learning, users are partitioned into K clients. We consider IID partition and non-IID partition. For non-IID simulation, we adopt a Dirichlet distribution [36] with concentration parameter $\alpha \in \{0.1, 0.3, 1.0\}$. Smaller α corresponds to more severe data heterogeneity, while $\alpha = 1.0$ represents moderate skew.

Baselines. We compare the proposed method against centralized, federated non-graph, and federated graph recommendation models.

Centralized Models. We first consider classical collaborative filtering baselines trained in a centralized manner. **MF** [8] learns low-dimensional latent representations for users and items and models their interactions via inner products. **NCF** [7] replaces the linear interaction in MF with a multi-layer perceptron to capture non-linear user–item relationships. **LightGCN** [6] propagates embeddings on the user–item bipartite graph without feature transformation, effectively modeling high-order collaborative signals.

Federated Non-Graph Models. To evaluate the impact of federated learning without graph modeling, we include several collaborative baselines under distributed training. **FedMF** [3] extends matrix factorization to the federated setting, where user representations are updated locally and item parameters are aggregated globally. **FedNCF** [18] adapts neural collaborative filtering to decentralized environments by sharing item-related parameters while keeping user embeddings local. **PFedRec** [38] introduces personalization by separating shared and client-specific components. **FedRecon** [21] reconstructs local representations during each communication round to enhance personalization under heterogeneous data.

Federated Graph Models. We further compare with state-of-the-art federated graph recommendation approaches. **FedLightGCN** extends LightGCN [6] to federated learning via parameter aggregation across clients. **GPFedRec** [39] leverages graph-guided aggregation strategies to improve cross-client structural knowledge transfer. **UFGraphFR** [25] integrates textual user features to construct similarity-aware user graphs in federated environments. **GFed-PP** [16] focuses on personalized federated graph learning to mitigate representation drift under non-IID settings.

Implementation Details. Embedding dimension is set to $d = 64$, and the number of graph propagation layers is $L_g = 2$. We use the Adam optimizer with learning rate 10^{-3}. Each communication round consists of five local training epochs. Adaptive community abstraction is performed using HDBSCAN with minimum cluster size of 10. The number of representative items per community is set to $L = 10$. The semantic encoder is a frozen pretrained language model, and semantic embeddings are ℓ_2-normalized before similarity computation. We keep the semantic encoder fixed in order to avoid additional synchronization and communication overhead during federated training. Hyperparameters λ, λ_{align}, and δ are tuned using validation sets.

5.2   RQ1: Overall Performance

Table 1 presents the overall performance under the non-IID setting ($\alpha = 0.3$). Among all baselines, UFGraphFR achieves the strongest results: 75.7% (HR@10) and 47.0% (NDCG@10) on MovieLens-100K; 75.2% and 46.0% on MovieLens-1M; and 81.8% and 72.6% on Amazon-Video. In comparison, SemFGRec consistently delivers the best performance, achieving 77.7% and 49.0%, 77.3% and

Table 1. Overall performance comparison under the non-IID setting ($\alpha = 0.3$). Best results are in **bold** and the best baseline results are underlined.

Group	Method	MovieLens-100K		MovieLens-1M		Amazon-Video	
		HR@10	NDCG@10	HR@10	NDCG@10	HR@10	NDCG@10
CenRec	MF	64.6	38.8	68.9	41.7	47.2	30.4
	NCF	64.9	38.3	64.7	38.3	60.6	39.2
	LightGCN	64.3	37.4	60.9	33.9	60.4	39.3
FedRec	FedMF	65.1	39.3	68.0	41.0	59.7	38.6
	FedNCF	60.9	34.2	60.7	34.3	57.9	36.9
	PFedRec	71.9	43.6	73.3	44.3	59.6	37.8
	FedRecon	64.8	38.3	63.5	38.8	58.8	38.1
	MetaMF	66.7	41.1	46.0	25.6	58.0	37.6
	FedLightGCN	23.8	12.7	36.7	14.9	56.1	34.9
	GPFedRec	72.5	43.4	72.7	43.9	58.6	38.4
	GFedPP	73.3	43.9	73.5	44.4	<u>82.2</u>	<u>73.0</u>
	UFGraphFR	<u>75.7</u>	<u>47.0</u>	<u>75.2</u>	<u>46.0</u>	81.8	72.6
Ours	SemFGRec	**77.7**	**49.0**	**77.3**	**48.0**	**83.5**	**74.3**

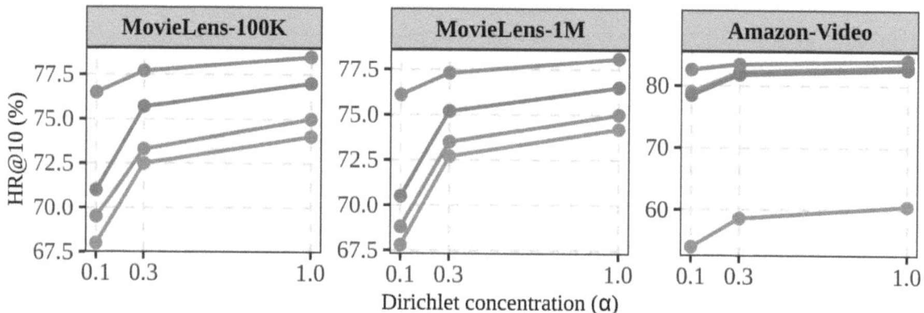

Fig. 2. HR@10 (%) under different levels of data heterogeneity ($\alpha \in \{0.1, 0.3, 1.0\}$). Smaller α indicates more severe non-IID distributions.

48.0%, and 83.5% and 74.3% on the respective datasets. These correspond to absolute improvements of approximately two percentage points in both metrics over the strongest baseline, demonstrating superior robustness under heterogeneous client distributions.

5.3 RQ2: Robustness Under Non-IID Settings

Figure 2 presents HR@10 under varying degrees of client heterogeneity. As α decreases from 1.0 to 0.1, representative baselines such as UFGraphFR drop

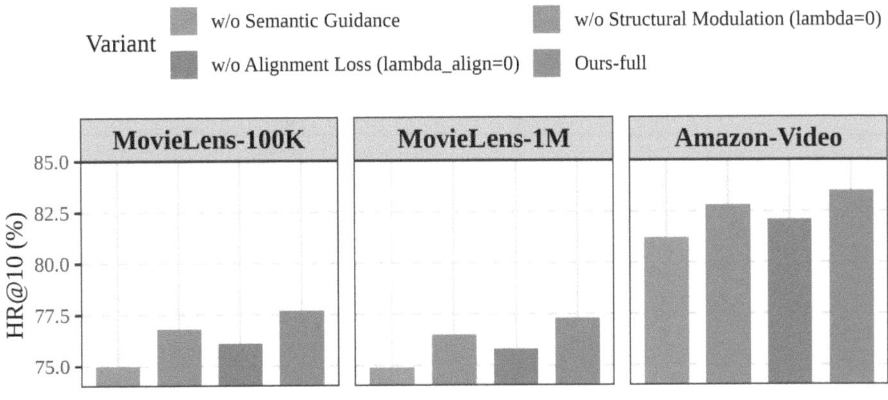

Fig. 3. Ablation study on HR@10 (%) under the non-IID setting ($\alpha = 0.3$).

notably (e.g., 77.0% to 71.0% on MovieLens-100K), indicating sensitivity to non-IID distributions. In contrast, `SemFGRec` shows much smaller degradation: 78.5% to 76.5% on MovieLens-100K, and 78.1% to 76.1% on MovieLens-1M. It consistently maintains the highest performance across all α values. These results demonstrate that the semantic-first merging strategy effectively stabilizes cross-client aggregation under heterogeneous settings.

5.4   RQ3: Ablation Study

Figure 3 reports the contribution of each component under the non-IID setting ($\alpha = 0.3$). Removing semantic guidance leads to the largest performance drop across all datasets; for example, HR@10 decreases from 77.7% to 75.0% on MovieLens-100K and from 83.5% to 81.2% on Amazon-Video. Disabling the alignment loss also degrades performance (e.g., 77.7%→76.1% on MovieLens-100K), while removing structural modulation ($\lambda_{\mathrm{merge}} = 0$) results in a smaller but consistent reduction. These results indicate that semantic-first merging is the most critical component, and that both structural modulation and alignment-aware optimization contribute to the overall effectiveness of the framework.

5.5   RQ4: Hyperparameter Sensitivity

Figure 4 shows that `SemFGRec` is stable across a broad range of hyperparameter values. For the structural modulation weight, performance improves from 76.8% at $\lambda = 0$ to a peak of 77.7% at $\lambda = 1$, and remains competitive even for larger values (e.g., 77.49% at $\lambda = 8$). Similarly, the alignment weight exhibits a clear sweet spot: HR@10 rises from 76.1% at $\lambda_{\mathrm{align}} = 0$ to 77.7% at $\lambda_{\mathrm{align}} = 10^{-3}$, and varies only mildly thereafter (e.g., 77.53% at $\lambda_{\mathrm{align}} = 5 \times 10^{-3}$). Overall, the method is not overly sensitive to tuning, indicating robust behavior with respect to key hyperparameters.

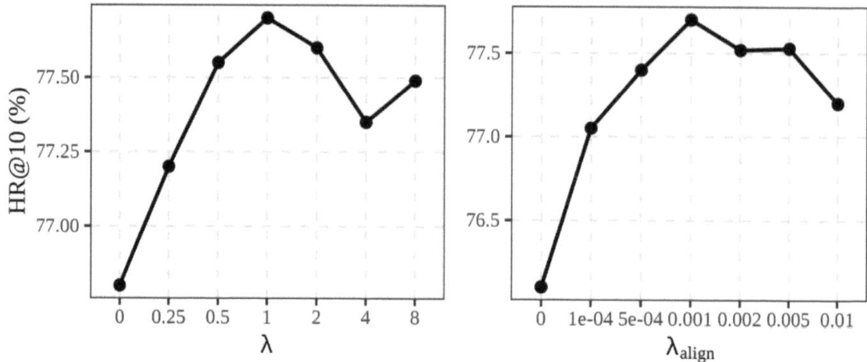

Fig. 4. Sensitivity analysis of the structural modulation weight λ and the alignment weight λ_{align} on MovieLens-100K under the non-IID setting ($\alpha = 0.3$), measured by HR@10 (%).

6   Conclusion

This paper presents a semantic–structural federated graph recommendation framework to mitigate representation misalignment under non-IID client distributions. Instead of relying solely on structural parameter aggregation, the proposed approach introduces community-level abstraction and semantic-first merging to regulate cross-client collaboration. By constructing structural prototypes from local interaction graphs and guiding their alignment using LLM-derived semantic representations, the framework enables effective knowledge transfer while keeping raw interaction data local. Experimental results demonstrate consistent improvements over strong federated and graph-based baselines under heterogeneous settings, and confirm the stability of the method across different hyperparameter configurations.

For future work, we plan to conduct a comprehensive system-level evaluation of the framework, including communication cost per round, runtime performance, and CPU/GPU resource usage under different deployment settings. We also aim to explore large-scale distributed deployment scenarios to better understand scalability and system behavior under realistic network and client heterogeneity. In addition, dynamic semantic updating strategies and more efficient community representation mechanisms will be investigated to further improve adaptability and system efficiency.

References

1. Ammad-Ud-Din, M., et al.: Federated collaborative filtering for privacy-preserving personalized recommendation system. arXiv (2019)
2. Campello, R.J., Moulavi, D., Sander, J.: Density-based clustering based on hierarchical density estimates. In: PAKDD, pp. 160–172 (2013)

3. Chai, D., Wang, L., Chen, K., Yang, Q.: Secure federated matrix factorization. IEEE Intell. Syst. **36**(5), 11–20 (2020)
4. Chen, Q., Wang, Z., Yan, M., Yan, H., Lin, X., Zhou, J.: DefedGCN: privacy-preserving decentralized federated GCN for recommender system. TSC **18**(2), 729–742 (2025)
5. Harper, F.M., Konstan, J.A.: The movielens datasets: history and context. ACM TiiS **5**(4), 1–19 (2015)
6. He, X., Deng, K., Wang, X., Li, Y., Zhang, Y., Wang, M.: LightGCN: simplifying and powering graph convolution network for recommendation. In: SIGIR, pp. 639–648 (2020)
7. He, X., Liao, L., Zhang, H., Nie, L., Hu, X., Chua, T.S.: Neural collaborative filtering. In: WWW, pp. 173–182 (2017)
8. Koren, Y., Bell, R., Volinsky, C.: Matrix factorization techniques for recommender systems. Computer **42**(8), 30–37 (2009)
9. Kumar, C., Alam, M.: An in-depth analysis of recommender systems for integration of knowledge graphs utilising federated XAI model. Int. J. Inf. Technol. **17**(5), 3147–3155 (2025)
10. Liu, Z., Yang, L., Fan, Z., Peng, H., Yu, P.S.: Federated social recommendation with graph neural network. TIST **13**(4), 1–24 (2022)
11. Long, J., Chen, T., Ye, G., Zheng, K., Nguyen, Q.V.H., Yin, H.: Physical trajectory inference attack and defense in decentralized poi recommendation. In: WWW, pp. 3379–3387 (2024)
12. Long, J., Ye, G., Chen, T., Wang, Y., Wang, M., Yin, H.: Diffusion-based cloud-edge-device collaborative learning for next poi recommendations. In: KDD, pp. 2026–2036 (2024)
13. Lyu, H., et al.: LLM-rec: Personalized recommendation via prompting large language models. In: NAACL, pp. 583–612 (2024)
14. Ma, X., Zhang, H., Zeng, J., Duan, Y., Wen, X.: FedKGRec: privacy-preserving federated knowledge graph aware recommender system: X. Ma et al. Appl. Intell. **54**(19), 9028–9044 (2024)
15. Mai, P., Pang, Y.: Vertical federated graph neural network for recommender system. In: ICML, pp. 23516–23535 (2023)
16. Na, C., et al.: Graph federated learning for personalized privacy recommendation. arXiv (2025)
17. Ni, J., Li, J., McAuley, J.: Justifying recommendations using distantly-labeled reviews and fine-grained aspects. In: EMNLP-IJCNLP, pp. 188–197 (2019)
18. Perifanis, V., Efraimidis, P.S.: Federated neural collaborative filtering. KBS **242**, 108441 (2022)
19. Qi, Q., Hu, C., Li, T., Tang, P., Guo, S.: PFGRS: a privacy-preserving subgraph-level federated graph learning for recommender system. ESWA **282**, 127615 (2025)
20. Qu, L., Yuan, W., Zheng, R., Cui, L., Shi, Y., Yin, H.: Towards personalized privacy: user-governed data contribution for federated recommendation. In: WWW, pp. 3910–3918 (2024)
21. Singhal, K., Sidahmed, H., Garrett, Z., Wu, S., Rush, J., Prakash, S.: Federated reconstruction: partially local federated learning. In: NeurIPS, vol. 34, pp. 11220–11232 (2021)
22. Soyarar, E., Aydogan, R., Buzcu, B., Calvaresi, D.: Explaining federated learning-based movie recommendations. In: MetroXRAINE, pp. 729–734. IEEE (2025)
23. Tan, G.: NAH-GNN: a graph-based framework for multi-behavior and high-hop interaction recommendation. PLoS ONE **20**(4), e0321419 (2025)

24. Tang, Z., Huan, Z., Li, Z., Zhang, X., Hu, J., Fu, C., Zhou, J., Zou, L., Li, C.: One model for all: large language models are domain-agnostic recommendation systems. TOIS **43**(5), 1–27 (2025)
25. Wang, X., Hao, Q., Cheng, X., Xiao, Y.: UFGraphFR: graph federation recommendation system based on user text description features. arXiv (2025)
26. Wu, C., Wu, F., Lyu, L., Qi, T., Huang, Y., Xie, X.: A federated graph neural network framework for privacy-preserving personalization. Nat. Commun. **13**(1), 3091 (2022)
27. Wu, L., et al.: A survey on large language models for recommendation. WWW **27**(5), 60 (2024)
28. Xu, Z., Li, B., Cao, W.: Enhancing federated learning-based social recommendations with graph attention networks. Neurocomputing **617**, 129045 (2025)
29. Yang, Z., et al.: Federated graph learning for cross-domain recommendation. In: NeurIPS, vol. 37, pp. 64865–64888 (2024)
30. Yao, Y., et al.: Federated large language models: current progress and future directions (2024)
31. Ye, R., et al.: FedLLM-bench: realistic benchmarks for federated learning of large language models (2024)
32. Yin, H., et al.: On-device recommender systems: a comprehensive survey. Data Sci. Eng. 1–30 (2025)
33. Yuan, W., Qu, L., Cui, L., Tong, Y., Zhou, X., Yin, H.: HeteFedRec: federated recommender systems with model heterogeneity. In: ICDE, pp. 1324–1337 (2024)
34. Yuan, W., Yang, C., Qu, L., Nguyen, Q.V.H., Li, J., Yin, H.: Hide your model: a parameter transmission-free federated recommender system. In: ICDE, pp. 611–624 (2024)
35. Yuan, W., Yang, C., Ye, G., Chen, T., Nguyen, Q.V.H., Yin, H.: FELLAS: enhancing federated sequential recommendation with LLM as external services. TOIS **43**(6), 1–24 (2025)
36. Yurochkin, M., Agarwal, M., Ghosh, S., Greenewald, K., Hoang, N., Khazaeni, Y.: Bayesian nonparametric federated learning of neural networks. In: ICML, pp. 7252–7261 (2019)
37. Zeng, H., Yue, Z., Jiang, Q., Wang, D.: Federated recommendation via hybrid retrieval augmented generation. In: BigData, pp. 8078–8087. IEEE (2024)
38. Zhang, C., et al.: Dual personalization on federated recommendation. arXiv (2023)
39. Zhang, C., Long, G., Zhou, T., Zhang, Z., Yan, P., Yang, B.: GPFedRec: graph-guided personalization for federated recommendation. In: KDD, pp. 4131–4142 (2024)
40. Zhao, J., Wang, W., Xu, C., Ng, S.K., Chua, T.S.: A federated framework for LLM-based recommendation. In: NAACL, pp. 2852–2865 (2025)

Storage and Distributed Systems

Graph-Matrix Model for Data Storage Systems

Quentin Voiret[2(✉)] , Bertrand Ducourthial[2] , Pascal Felber[1] ,
and Valerio Schiavoni[1]

[1] University of Neuchâtel, Neuchâtel, Switzerland
{pascal.felber,valerio.schiavoni}@unine.ch
[2] Université de Technologie de Compiègne, Compiègne, France
{quentin.voiret,bertrand.ducourthial}@utc.fr

Abstract. The amount of data generated each year continues to increase. Some of this data must be preserved, and this becomes a significant issue when critical data are involved. Data storage systems must protect against risks that affect both data and infrastructure (primarily the storage media). To fulfil this requirement, the system should offer both data versioning (to restore previous safe versions) and replication (to mitigate device failures). These two functions should be dimensioned based on risk analysis, which may, however, result in complex software/hardware architectures. In this paper, we propose a simple graph model that accounts for risks to both data and devices and facilitates the design of a data storage system. It is complemented by a matrix model that allows analysis of specific properties. The proposed models enable the detection of suboptimal architectures and facilitate understanding of the operations of the backup system. In addition, this study can also support future work on risk management in backup systems.

Keywords: data storage · backup strategies · system model

1 Introduction

The global volume of data generated continues to grow, reaching 149 zettabytes (ZB) in 2024, according to Statista [3]. Additionally, 2% of this data must be saved [23]. This amount of data is impressive, and storage infrastructures must be properly sized to ensure resilience while minimizing their environmental impact. Thus, resilience presents a significant challenge for data storage systems. Although they require data replication (multiple copies) and historization (multiple versions) to ensure reliability, these measures can increase both storage usage and environmental impact. Designing such a system requires balancing resilience with storage efficiency, as these two metrics are directly linked to the risks threatening the system. In fact, there are many scenarios in which it is necessary to recover the data [5]. A well-designed system can mitigate these risks by balancing storage overhead with reliability requirements.

The consequences of systems with implementation problems can be severe. For example, Toy Story 2 was nearly lost during production due to a system

A. Nunes Alonso and R. Palmieri (Eds.): DAIS 2026, LNCS 16591, pp. 55–71, 2026.
https://doi.org/10.1007/978-3-032-27358-1_4

command error. It was recovered thanks to a personal copy that an employee had kept at home [19]. Even in a system with backups, data loss can occur, such as when Dedoose lost both data and backups after a crash [20]. Such incidents continue to happen. In 2023, the Iowa hospital suffered a data breach after falling victim to the Royal ransomware attack [27]. In 2025, South Korea's government lost 858 TB of data in a fire, due to a lack of backups and replications [21]. In addition to data loss, availability is a critical factor, leading to the combination of local and remote solutions. For example, major cloud providers such as AWS [10] and Azure [11] experienced failures that resulted in significant outages across various applications.

Generally, data storage refers to the primary data source linked to a computational facility and/or the secondary data source(s) used as a backup to restore the primary source in case of data loss [24]. We focus on the system as a whole, called *Data Storage System* (DSS). A DSS comprises devices that store data and additional components for data transfer, among other functions.

The overview [9] showed that, in general, a DSS provides protection against a wide range of threats, including device failure, viruses, malicious damage, volume and directory errors, transfer corruption, natural disasters (*e.g.*, lightning strike, fire, water damage), theft, and human error. Any system under one of these threats needs a robust backup system. Studying and representing a DSS can help identify weaknesses in its architecture. This analysis enables the detection of potential vulnerabilities with previous threats and the implementation of measures to improve system reliability and efficiency.

This paper presents a model for studying DSSs that combines two complementary approaches: a graph model to visualise data flow and backup relationships, with a novel matrix model that quantifies version availability across system components. Our graph model provides an intuitive understanding of backup operations by clearly depicting the hierarchical structure of the system, the flow of data between components, and the temporal relationships between backup operations. Meanwhile, the matrix model complements this graph view by enabling precise computation of key metrics that are not directly visible on the graph. Specifically, it enables one to calculate the exact number of versions available for each component of the system, assess coverage across different backup frequencies, and identify potential gaps in version availability that could compromise data recovery. These representations enable a better study and sizing of DSS, thereby contributing to more efficient resource management, which in turn reduces their environmental impacts. Our approach can be combined with data coding techniques (*e.g.*, erasure codes, RAID) to optimise the use of storage capacities, at the price of additional communication and processing costs upon recovery. Such techniques are orthogonal to our model and are not explicitly addressed in this paper.

This paper is organised as follows. Section 2 formalises the role of backups, recommendations, and common backup architectures. Section 3 details our graph model methodology. Section 4 explores our matrix model. We discuss our approaches in Sect. 5, before concluding and discussing future work in Sect. 6.

Table 1. Threat assessment of an information system and the efficacy of replication and backup

Threat	Is device or data at risk?	Is replication effective?	Is backup effective?
Employee deletes files	Data	No	Yes
Technician smashes server	Device	Yes	No
Trojan horse, worm, logic bomb	Data	No	Yes
Ransomware	Data	No	Yes
Errors and omissions	Data	No	Yes
Loss of physical infrastructure or support	Device	Yes	No

2   State of the Art

In this paper, we focus on data backup and solutions to mitigate data loss in DSS. Given their vital role, there are now recommendations for their implementation. We discuss them further in the following.

2.1   Role of Backup

When designing a DSS, it is crucial to identify potential threats that could damage or make it unavailable. Data loss remains a critical challenge that requires robust backup strategies. However, existing approaches face a trade-off: strong recoverability has to be reached without an excessive use of storage resources. Vulnerabilities can arise from management or operational weaknesses and can potentially cause significant damage when exploited. These threats define risk, measured by the severity and probability of negative impacts [6]. There is a distinction between threats with or without an adversary [18]. Table 1 summarises these threats, distinguishing between risks to data (where backups enable recovery of previous versions) and risks to devices (where replication ensures redundancy across multiple storage units).

2.2   Recommendations

To reduce risks in a DSS, several recommendations have been established and must be followed. Firstly, there is the 3-2-1 backup rule, as defined by ANSSI [1], which requires maintaining 3 copies of the data, using 2 different media, one of which must be kept offline. However, there is a lack of understanding about the definition: NIST [17] defines the "1" as one off-site copy, whereas ANSSI requires it to be offline. Other organizations [15] recommend having one copy off-site.

Moreover, ANSSI recommends retaining data for a specified period, depending on the backup frequency. For example, 15 days of daily backups, 1 year of monthly backups, and 5 years of annual backups.

Complementary guidelines include Techtarget's eight critical backup practices [25], which extend the 3-2-1 rule. These practices emphasise aligning backup frequency with service-level demands, judicious use of cloud backups, automation of disaster recovery procedures, secure endpoint, and SaaS application protection. Similarly, the International Code of Conduct Association (ICoCA) [7] advocates implementing the 3-2-1 rule, encrypting backups, regularly testing recovery processes, and developing comprehensive disaster recovery plans.

2.3   Common Examples of DSS

There are three primary backup methods [8]. A *full backup* copies all data, ensuring completeness at the cost of storage space and time. An *incremental backup* saves only modified data since the last backup (whether full or incremental), requiring the restoration of all backups since the last full one. A *differential backup* saves all changes since the last full backup, requiring restoration of only the last full backup and the last differential one. These methods optimize backups but still require replication and historization. For the sake of simplicity, this paper considers full backups. Several architectures exist for DSS, offering a wide range of configurations to model. The *hierarchical system* links storage units in a chain with increasing data storage size. The *cyclic system* connects the source directly to all storage units, using them sequentially. The *Grandfather-Father-Son (GFS) system* [16] is a cyclic system that assigns unique periodicities to each storage unit. The *Hanoi Tower system* [4,22] associates each storage unit with one of the puzzle pieces. The storage unit is used to back up data at the same periodicity as the corresponding piece is moved to solve the puzzle. The *sneakernet system* uses an external device (*e.g.*, USB key) connected only during backup.

Backup strategies can be extended [15]. The *3-2-1 rule* from NIST leads to the *3-1-2 rule* and the *3-2-2 rule*. Both cases require 2 offsite copies. The former keeps them in the cloud, while the latter uses a physical storage unit. The *3-2-1-1-0* is an extension of the *3-2-1* strategy from NIST with an offline, air-gapped, or immutable copy ("1") and integrity verification ("0"). Big corporations also implement their method. Microsoft Azure Backup [14] integrates with Data Protection Manager (DPM) and Microsoft Azure Backup Server (MABS) through the Azure Recovery Services (MARS) agent. This agent performs daily backups to an Azure Recovery Services vault, complementing the hourly local backups handled by DPM/MABS protection agents. This hybrid approach combines cloud-based disaster recovery with on-premises protection.

Research contributions include an optimisation model [13] that combines full and incremental backups to restore the closest pre-disaster version of the data. Another study [2] proposes a backup model for digital learning platforms using a 4-week cycle (weekly full backups with daily incremental backups) and local/remote replication. The study [26] highlights undetected storage errors and proposes erasure coding for mitigation. Finally, authors [12] suggest combining backup systems with preventive replacement in standby systems to avoid unexpected errors.

2.4   Problem Statement

Modelling a DSS. Our review of the literature revealed that there is no formal method for representing DSS. However, a standardised model offers significant advantages. First, it would facilitate objective comparisons between different DSSs, enabling quick identification of systems that best meet specific requirements. Second, a clear model also raises awareness of good practices among corporate employees. Third, a well-defined model would provide a persuasive argument, making it easier to gain the approval and support of the stakeholders.

Evaluation of a DSS. When considering a DSS, two key questions arise. First, regarding in-width use: how many different data elements does the DSS contain? This question addresses version counts, providing information about recoverable copies. The DSS architecture should optimise the number of different copies based on available storage supports and corporate needs. Second, with respect to recovery time: what is the relationship between saving periods and the oldest available version? This question focuses on recovery capability after failures. Even with many copies, there are still risks of failure propagation. In worst-case scenarios, the only available version might be the oldest, necessitating compliance with system-defined requirements for data age.

3   Graph Model of a DSS

This section features a simple visual model of the DSS. We begin by analysing key characteristics of DSS, then we introduce the graph model with common examples.

3.1   Threats and Distances

DSS must address threats to both data and storage devices. Data threats are mitigated through *backups*, enabling versioning and recovery of previous versions. Device threats (*e.g.*, building fires) are countered by *replication* using devices outside the affected area. DSS combines both strategies for comprehensive protection. The system's *source* is the computing unit that generates new data.

When assessing a remote copy u' of data u in a DSS, it is essential to quantify both the temporal and spatial intervals between the original and its replica. We define these intervals as follows:

Definition 1. *The* epoch *between a data u and its copy u', denoted $e(u, u')$, is the threat-relative temporal distance between them. It defines the time interval before corruption in u affects its copy u'.*

Definition 2. *The* gap *between a data u and its copy u', denoted $g(u, u')$, is the threat-relative spatial distance between them. It defines the geographical area that must be compromised to simultaneously affect both u and its copy u'.*

Table 2. Examples of spatial-relative distances for mitigating risks on devices

Gap	Example: Copy on ...	Mitigated risk
Filesystem	...the same file system	Writing error
Disk	...another partition of the same disk	File system error
Computer	...another drive on the same computer	Hard drive failure
Table	...an external drive on the same table	Computer failure
Room	...another device elsewhere in the room	Accidental liquid spill
Floor	...another device on another room	Theft
Building	...another device on another (higher) floor	Flooding
Campus	...another device on another building	Fire, lightning ...
Country	...another city in the same country	Natural or industrial disaster, armed conflict
Continent	...another country in the same continent	Major disaster, war, geopolitical risk
Earth	...another continent	Regional war, major nuclear disaster

For a given DSS, the epoch and gap values depend on the criticality of the data and must be determined through risk analysis.

Table 2 presents a non-proportional scale of spatial threat-related distances to mitigate device risks. Flood-prone areas are at risk of damaging ground-floor equipment, while buildings can be affected by fires, lightning, or burglary. Off-campus storage mitigates these risks. Natural and industrial disasters (*e.g.*, Fukushima) can destroy or block access to equipment. Larger gaps reduce environmental risks. Armed conflicts (*e.g.*, 9/11, Syrian Civil War) may lead to evacuations or destruction. Storing data in another country reduces the risks of major disasters (*e.g.*, tsunamis, war) and geopolitical threats (*e.g.*, 2022 Russian invasion of Ukraine). A nuclear disaster could destroy an entire region.

Table 3 lists examples of common epochs. Temporal constraints influence backup periods. The ASAP epoch ensures immediate remote reporting upon local writing, with delays depending on network conditions. Increasing the epoch protects against undetected threats (*e.g.*, data corruption). For example, a daily backup epoch may miss corruption within 24 h, requiring the retention of older backups (spanning days or weeks). Similarly, increasing the gap reduces environmental risks.

3.2   Graph Model

We propose a graph model of DSS that incorporates their key characteristics. Devices are treated as finite permanent storage units, represented indifferently as a hard drive (Fig. 1). The unit size may vary for the sake of clarity, with its identifier displayed in the hard drive icon. Additional parameters can be added below when needed (Fig. 1-middle). The minimal DSS configuration consists of a single unit: the source itself (Fig. 1-right).

Table 3. Examples of time-relative distance for mitigating risks on data

Epoch	Example
ASAP	Synchronous copy
Minutely	Critical systems
Several times per hour	15 min. for MS SQL Server on DPM or MABS
Hourly	Apple Time Machine
Several times per day	3 daily backups for MARS agent, 2 for DPM/MABS
Daily	Operational data
Weekly	Archival data
Monthly	Financial closing
Yearly	Historical traceability

Fig. 1. A node represents a storage unit containing data. Left: NAS storage unit. Middle: Write Once Read Multiple storage unit A. Right: source storage unit named PC.

Data transfer between DSS units is represented by directional edges (Fig. 2-left). Offline devices (connected only during data transfer) are shown with dashed edges (Fig. 2-middle). Additional parameters such as restoration delay may appear below the edge (Fig. 2-right).

Fig. 2. Directional edges indicate the sense of the data transfer. Left: disk 1 is backed up to disk 2, which is permanently connected. Middle: disk 2 is connected only during data transfer. Right: data recovery from disk 2 requires 3 h.

Edge labels indicate the transfer epoch, which can be a period of time or a periodic date (Fig. 3).

Fig. 3. Edges labels indicate either a period or a (periodic) date.

A dotted box indicates the shared risk gap between data units. For example, on Fig. 4-left, the PC and the disk share common risks (fire, theft) as they are located on the same desk. In Fig. 4-right, data units D1, D2 and D3 share device failure risks because they are stored on the same drive. A FIFO strategy uses multiple backups on a single drive with FIFO management: when space runs out, the oldest backup is deleted. This configuration is shown in Fig. 4-right, where the drive contains several units.

3.3   Application to Common DSS

We illustrate the proposed graph model with common DSS examples.

Personal System: An employee uses a computer with daily backups on an external disk (Fig. 4-left). This DSS configuration consists of two storage units separated by a *daily* epoch: if a failure occurs during the workday, the system can restore the previous day's backup from the external drive. When the employee retains the last backup copies on the disk, the DSS is represented as in Fig. 4-right. Here both units remain exposed to the same environmental risks associated with the shared desk (e.g., coffee spills or theft).

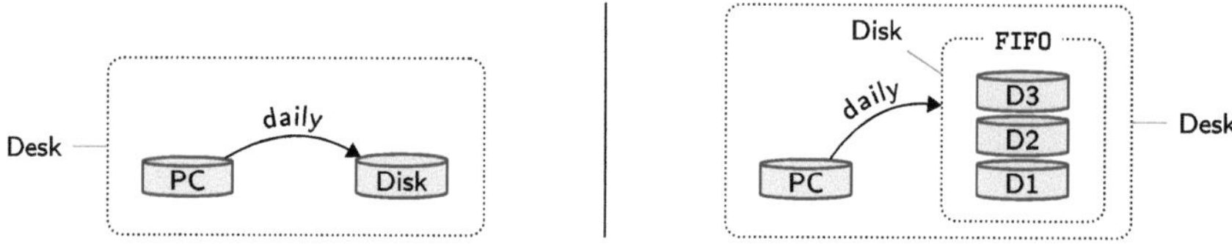

Fig. 4. Left: PC backed up daily to an external drive within the Desk gap; both share the risks associated with the Desk. Right: The external drive retains the three most recent backup copies, which share the Disk risks.

The remaining risks can still be mitigated by implementing weekly backups to a server located elsewhere in the Campus (Fig. 5-left). When working from home, the employee uses a USB key with the sneakernet method, increasing the gap to the City (Fig. 5-right).

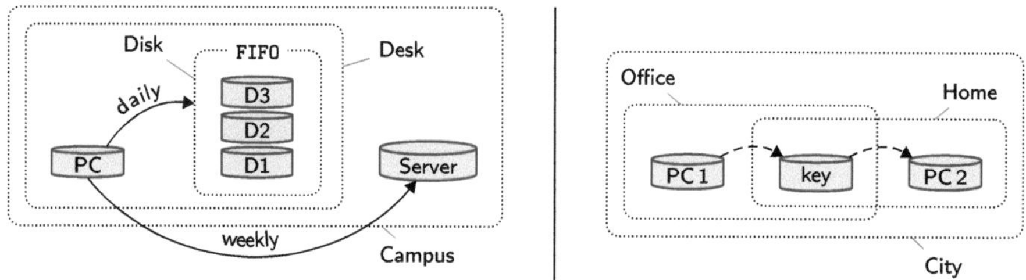

Fig. 5. Left: PC saved in an external drive and in a server. Right: PC saved following the sneakernet backup between *Office* and *Home*.

A DSS is nested when its gaps do not intersect as in Fig. 5-left or Fig. 8. To the contrary, DSS in Fig. 5-right or Fig. 11 are not nested.

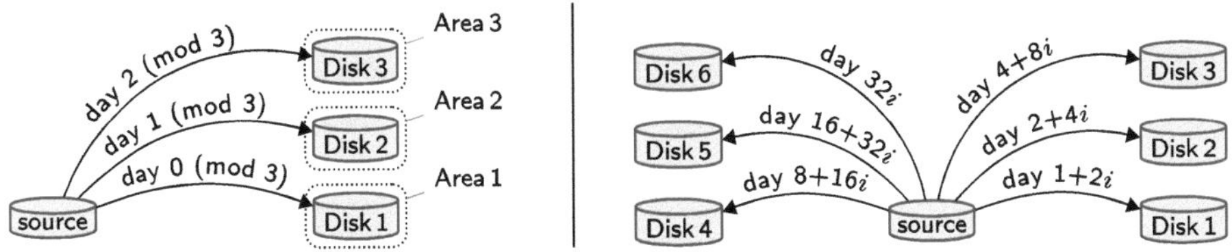

Fig. 6. Left: Cyclic DSS relying on three disks. Right: Hanoi DSS with $N = 6$ disks.

Cyclic DSS: A cyclic DSS uses multiple drives, possibly with different gaps, in rotation during backups to protect against drive failure (Fig. 6-left). While a cyclic DSS with N drives is similar to a FIFO DSS (Fig. 4-right) with one drive containing N backups, the FIFO system stores all copies on a single drive, risking total loss in case of failure. In contrast, a cyclic DSS maintains the availability of other drives if one fails. These strategies are often combined.

A *Hanoi* DSS is a cyclic DSS in which backup periods are fixed and defined according to the Hanoi Tower algorithm. With N drives, the backup involves drive k with $0 \le k < N$ every 2^k days starting from the 2^{k-1}-th day. An exception is made when $k = N$: the Nth drive is first saved on the 2^{k-1}-th day and then saved every 2^{k-1} days (see Table 4). This DSS is represented in Fig. 6-right.

Hierarchical and Path DSS: A DSS that relies on progressively larger devices that concentrate increasing amounts of data is qualified as *hierarchical*. For the sake of clarity, the nodes in the related DSS graph may be of different size. For example, Fig. 7 represents a hierarchical DSS based on Microsoft DPM/MABS (see Sect. 2). In contrast, the DSS of Fig. 5 that includes a USB key is not hierarchical. Most DSSs are hierarchical.

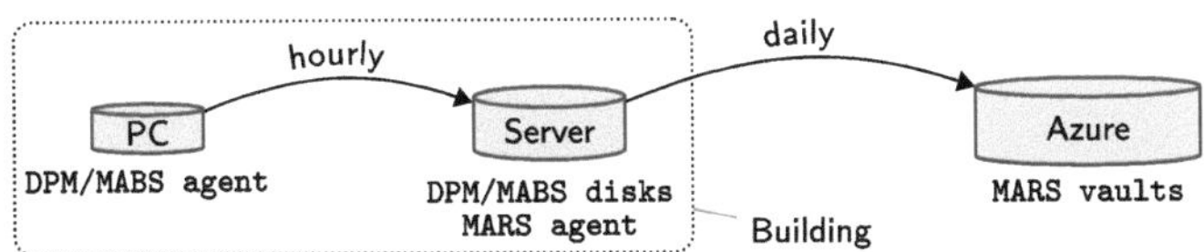

Fig. 7. PC saved following the Microsoft backup system.

Table 4. Hanoi tower DSS.

Disk number k	1 2 3 4 5 6
First save day 2^{k-1}	1 2 4 8 16 32
Period of saving in day 2^k	2 4 8 16 32 32

In general, a DSS graph is acyclic. A DSS represented by a path graph is said *path* DSS (Fig. 7). A DSS in which the final node of the path is divided into separate nodes, creating a branching structure, is also considered a *path* DSS if the separate nodes have the same periodicity (Fig. 8).

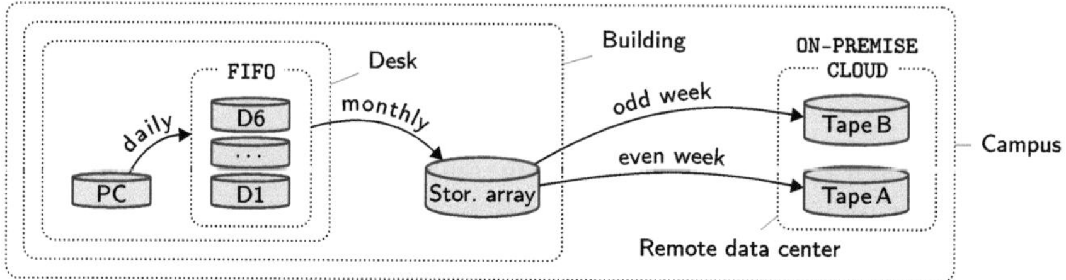

Fig. 8. Example of path DSS with multiple nodes at the last level which have the same periodicity.

Grand-father, Father, Son: A GFS DSS combines the cyclic and FIFO strategies. It relies on several cyclic systems with increasing periodicities $\tau_1 < \tau_2 < \tau_3$, such as daily, weekly, and monthly. Each cycle uses a FIFO strategy to keep several successive backups. Figure 9 displays a GFS DSS with daily, weekly, and monthly periods.

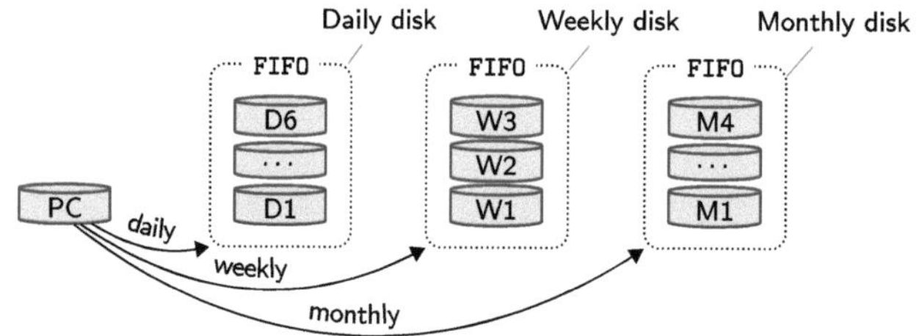

Fig. 9. Grand-father, father, son DSS.

3-2-1 DSS: The 3-2-1 saving method explicitly indicates the use of two different storage media, with one explicitly off-site, for the 3-2-1 method from NIST (Fig. 10-left) or offline, for the 3-2-1 method from ANSSI (Fig. 10-center).

The 3-2-1-1-0 saving system is an extension of the 3-2-1 approach. The graph is very similar, except that there is either one backup off-site and one backup offline, or one backup off-site and offline (Fig. 10-right).

3.4 Complete Example

To illustrate the capabilities of our graph model, let consider a fictional DSS example. The system features a PC with a RAID1 configuration (two mirrored drives). This PC is backed up weekly to a NAS located on the same desk. In addition, the IT department has implemented automatic hourly backups to a server

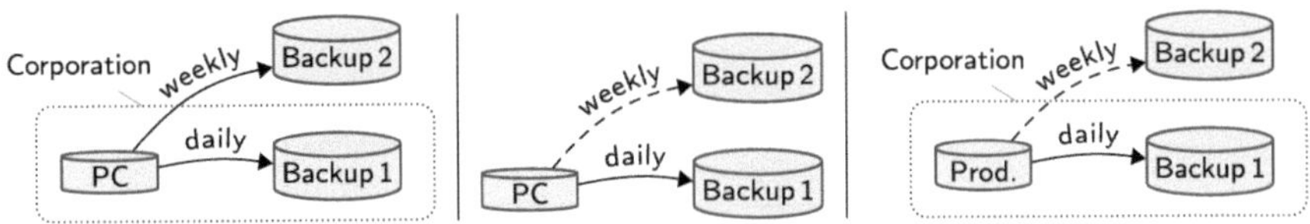

Fig. 10. Left: PC saved following the 3-2-1 backup system from NIST. Center: PC saved following the 3-2-1 backup system from ANSSI. Right: PC saved following the 3-2-1-1-0 backup system.

on the LAN. This server is then backed up daily to an on-premises cloud located in another campus building. The cloud is subsequently backed up weekly to tapes using alternating media. In parallel, the PC user has set up daily synchronisation with an external cloud at the end of each workday to facilitate business travel. Finally, before each weekend, the user copies the files to a USB key for secure off-network work on a home PC. Figure 11 shows this fictional DSS, illustrating how even complex DSS configurations can be effectively represented using the proposed graph approach.

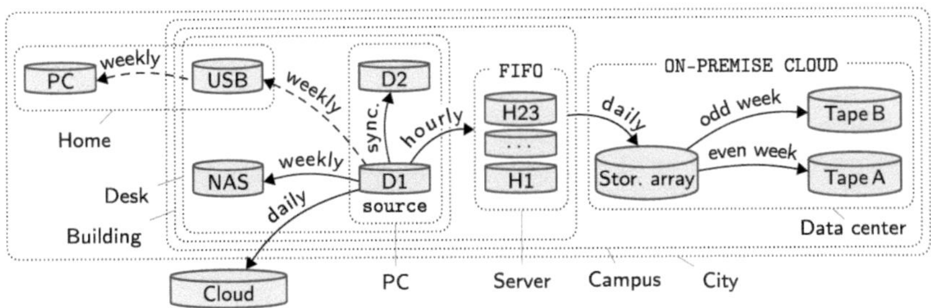

Fig. 11. Model of the fictional DSS example.

4 Matrix Model of DSS

As shown in the previous section, the proposed graph model effectively captures complex backup systems. We complement the graph model by introducing a matrix-based model approach that offers advantages such as comparisons between different implementations for a DSS, a fast way to detect non-optimal architecture, and the computation of some metrics for a DSS, as shown next.

4.1 Gap-Epoch Matrices

Consider a DSS A and its lists of epochs E_A and gaps G_A. Epochs of E_A are sorted in increasing order starting from the source epoch, which is considered

$$
\begin{array}{c}
\text{PC} \\ \text{Server} \\ \text{Azure}
\end{array}
\left(
\begin{array}{ccc}
1 & 0 & 0 \\
0 & 1 & 0 \\
0 & 0 & 1
\end{array}
\right)
\quad
\begin{array}{c}
\text{PC} \\ \text{desk} \\ \text{building} \\ \text{campus}
\end{array}
\left(
\begin{array}{cccc}
1 & 0 & 0 & 0 \\
0 & 6 & 0 & 0 \\
0 & 0 & 0 & 1 \\
0 & 0 & 2|2 & 0
\end{array}
\right)
\quad
\begin{array}{c}
\text{PC} \\ \text{desk} \\ \text{building} \\ \text{campus} \\ \text{city} \\ \text{cloud}
\end{array}
\left(
\begin{array}{cccc}
\frac{2}{2} & 0 & 0 & 0 \\
0 & 0 & 0 & \frac{2}{2} \\
0 & 23 & 0 & 0 \\
0 & 0 & 1 & 2|2 \\
0 & 0 & 0 & 1 \\
0 & 0 & 1 & 0
\end{array}
\right)
$$

Fig. 12. Gap-epoch matrices of DSS shown in Fig. 7, Fig. 8 and Fig. 11 respectively.

null by convention. Gaps are sorted from the inner, starting from the source, to the most encompassing. A gap that does not include the source is subsumed into the smallest gap that includes it. This defines a sorted sublist of G_A denoted G'_A. Using the sorted lists E_A and G'_A, we define functions e_A and g_A that return the ith epoch or gap, respectively, if it exists.

For example, in Fig. 11, E_A is "0" < "hourly" < "daily" < "weekly" and G'_A is "PC" ⊂ "Desk" ⊂ "Building" ⊂ "Campus" ⊂ "City". The gaps "Server", "Data center" and "Home" are included into "Building", "Campus" and "City" respectively. We then have $e_A(3) = $ "daily" and $g_A(1) = $ "PC".

Starting from e_A and g_A, we define the *gap-epoch matrix* of A as follows: this is an $n \times m$ matrix denoted M_A where the n rows correspond to sorted gaps and the m columns to the sorted epochs. Moreover, the element $M_A[i,j]$ can take three forms depending on the storage configuration. First, $M_A[i,j] = \frac{x}{y}$ when x copies are stored on y devices. Second, $M_A[i,j] = x|y$ when x copies are stored alternately on y devices. Finally, when a single storage unit is used for the gap $g_A(i)$ and epoch $e_A(j)$, the element simplifies to $M_A[i,j] = x/1 = x$, where x represents the number of versions stored in that unit.

For example, in the DSS shown in Fig. 11 and denoted A, where the PC uses RAID1 with two disks, we have $M_A[1,1] = \frac{2}{2}$. In the same DSS, where the "Storage array" is backed up every week alternately on "Tape 1" and "Tape 2", we have $M_A[4,4] = 2|2$. Figure 12 displays the gap-epoch matrix of some previously described DSSs.

4.2 Optimisation of the Number of Versions

The gap-epoch matrix helps identify non-optimal version counts for specific epochs in a DSS. Consider a system with s storage units and sorted epochs $p_1 < \cdots < p_{s-1}$. For each epoch p_i, we denote k_i as the number of versions. For example, in Fig. 9 (with $s = 4$), $p_1 = 1$ day, $p_2 = 1$ week, and $k_1 = 6$. We define $\hat{k}_i$ as:

$$\hat{k}_i = \left\lfloor \frac{p_{i+1}}{p_i} \right\rfloor - 1 \quad 0 < i < n \tag{1}$$

In case of data corruption, recovery depends on the detection delay. If corruption is detected after a given period, data are restored from versions in a higher epoch storage unit. For example, in Fig. 9, corruption detected after two days requires data restoration from daily copies. When $k_i < \hat{k}_i$, the storage unit i lacks sufficient versions to cover the epoch p_{i+1}, which requires data to be recovered from older copies in unit $i + 1$. For example, in Fig. 9, keeping only 4 daily versions may require restoring from weekly backups, increasing the restoration delay. In contrast, when $k_i > \hat{k}_i$, recovery remains unaffected, but storage usage increases. For example, in Fig. 9, keeping 10 daily versions could extend p_2 to 11 days instead of a week.

The value $\hat{k}_i$ ensures full version coverage between backups at epoch p_{i+1} without excessive storage use. Proper DSS sizing helps limit the environmental impact. This can be verified using the gap-epoch matrix. Considering a DSS A and its $n \times m$ gap-epoch matrix denoted M_A, if the backups occur at epoch $e_A(j)$ and gap $g_A(i)$, then $M_A[i, j]$ should be equal to $\hat{k}_j$ (Eq. 1) for every $i \in \{1, ..., n\}$ and $j \in \{2, ..., m - 1\}$.

4.3   Optimisation of the Epochs

The gap-epoch matrix also helps identify non-optimal epoch choices in *path* DSSs such as those in Fig. 7 and Fig. 8.

Consider a *path* DSS with s storage units and epochs $p_1, \ldots, p_{s-1}$. If the epochs are not increasing along the path, then it leads to a non-optimal solution with redundant backup operations. For example, in Fig. 8 p_1 is a day, p_2 is a month, p_3 and p_4 are a week modulo 2. In this configuration, $p_1 < p_2$ but $p_2 > p_3$ and $p_2 > p_4$. The weekly modulo 2 backups are identical for an entire month, until new data is saved in the monthly storage. On the contrary, epochs are increasing along the path in the DSS of Fig. 7.

Such a property can be easily observed in the gap-epoch matrix, where the non-zero values should draw a "descending staircase". This is not the case in Fig. 12-middle unlike Fig. 12-left. More formally, let M_A be a gap-epoch matrix for a path DSS A. For every $i \in \{1, ..., n - 1\}$ and $j \in \{1, ...m - 1\}$, if backups are made in epoch $e_A(j)$ and gap $g_A(i)$, then for all $i < k \le n$ and $1 \le l < j$, $M_A[k, l] = 0$.

4.4   Number of Copies

We define the number of copies for a given epoch as the largest value of the quotients of the corresponding column, except for the values of the form $x|y$ for which we consider the numerator value x since the x backups are different from each other. Taking into account a DSS A and its gap-epoch matrix M_A, we define $\mathrm{num}(M_A[i, j])$ as the value of the quotient or the numerator value for the notation $x|y$ associated with $M_A[i, j]$. Let us denote n_A^j the number of copies in epoch $e_A(j)$. Then:

$$n_A^j = \max_{1 \le i \le n} \mathrm{num}(M_A[i, j])$$

Once the number of copies is computed for each epoch, we obtain a bound on the total number of copies in the DSS A denoted n_A:

$$n_A \leq \sum_{j=1}^{m} n_A^j$$

If data is saved in no more than one epoch at any given time t, then the equality holds. For example, in the DSS shown in Fig. 11-right with its gap-epoch matrix presented in Fig. 12, the number of copies is 28.

4.5   Maximum Recovery Period

The oldest backup of a DSS determines the maximal detection period of corrupted data: after such a period, the entire DSS may be corrupted, preventing any recovery. For a given DSS A, this period denoted p_A is easily obtained thanks to its gap-epoch matrix M_A using the number of copies per epoch n_A^j previously defined:

$$p_A = \max_j \left(\left\lfloor n_A^j \times e_A(j) \right\rfloor \right)$$

In the matrix of Fig. 12-left, the maximum recovery period is 2 weeks, determined by the 2 weekly versions. However, if they were 20 daily versions instead of 1, the maximum delay would increase to 20 days. This shows that the maximum delay is not necessarily determined by the column with the largest epoch.

5   Discussion

Consider a corporation tasked with designing a DSS that mitigates risks to data and devices with three weeks of resilience (two weeks of fault detection and one week of system repair). It needs copies on another drive (PC), an external drive (Desk), and two servers distributed across the campus to address hardware failures and natural disasters (Table 2). In addition, synchronous, daily, and weekly backups ensure three weeks of resilience (Table 3).

From these requirements, the DSS must include the gaps "PC" $\subset$ "Desk" $\subset$ "Campus" and epochs "0" $<$ "daily" $<$ "weekly". Backups are made from the PC to the desk, then transferred to the two servers which are not in the same buildings. For daily backups, we apply the rule from Sect. 4.2 (6 versions), while weekly backups require at least 4 versions for three weeks of resilience. We have a *path* DSS; to avoid unnecessary operations, epochs should increase along the path (Sect. 4.3), with daily backups on the desk and weekly backups in both servers. The resulting gap-epoch matrix is shown in Fig. 13-left, assuming that weekly backups are made in both buildings.

The gap-epoch matrix can be used to construct a graph, although this model is not unique. Its accuracy depends solely on the DSS description's precision. In particular, with only the matrix on Fig. 13-left, we cannot determine whether

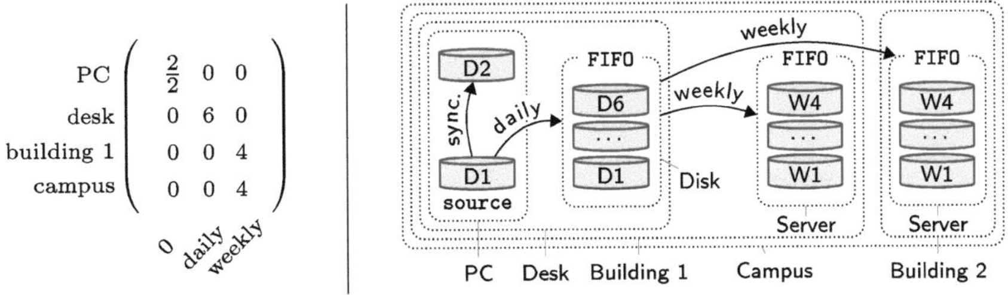

Fig. 13. Left: gap-epoch matrix M_A of the DSS A. Right: DSS satisfying the specifications, built from the gap-epoch matrix displayed on the left.

weekly server backups originate from the PC or desk, nor how they are distributed across the campus. According to our previous hypothesis, the corresponding DSS graph is shown in Fig. 13-right. Using the matrix, we obtain: $n_A = 11$ and $p_A = 4$ weeks.

6 Conclusion

This paper first emphasises the critical role of data backup, highlighting its fundamental importance in modern storage strategies to counteract data threats in DSS. Recommendations from government agencies [1,17], tech industry publications [25] and standards organisation [7] exist and should be followed when a DSS is implemented. The most representative implementations are presented.

To facilitate the presentation of DSS and the detection of issues within them, we introduce two models. Firstly, a graph model to visualise the data flow and backup relationships. Secondly, the gap-epoch matrix enables detection of non-optimal DSS and computation of key system metrics such as the number of copies and the maximum recovery period. Our approach highlights fundamental challenges for DSSs such as the trade-off between storage efficiency and the need for a formal method to evaluate system configurations.

These models demonstrate that the optimal configuration of the backup system is based on optimal choices for version counts and periodicities. Our contributions provide a framework for designing more efficient backup systems, thereby strengthening data protection in modern information systems. By allowing organisations to size the storage infrastructure, quantify risk levels in collaboration with IT teams, and align reliability targets with architectural requirements, our model offers a comprehensive approach to enhancing data resilience.

Future work will focus on refining the gap and epoch concepts. The study of the first one leads to a risk analysis of the system to specify which scale of gaps one should use. The second raises questions about the periodicities used to data backup and their corresponding lifetimes. This enhancement will improve the gap-epoch matrix model, enabling operations between them.

References

1. ANSSI: Sauvegarde des systèmes d'information. Technical report. Version 1.0, Agence nationale de la sécurité des systèmes d'information (ANSSI) (2023)
2. Ao, L.: Data storage architecture and data backup scheme for digital learning platform. In: 2023 IEEE International Conference on Control, Electronics and Computer Technology (ICCECT), pp. 1211–1215. (2023)
3. Bartley, K.: Big data statistics: how much data is there in the world? (2025). https://rivery.io/blog/big-data-statistics-how-much-data-is-there-in-the-world, consulté le 16 février 2026
4. Chervenak, A.L., Vellanki, V., Kurmas, Z.: Protecting file systems: a survey of backup techniques. In: Proceedings of the IEEE Symposium on Mass Storage Systems and Technologies (MSST) (1998). https://msstconference.org/MSST-history/1998/papers/a1-2-CHERVE.pdf
5. Fisher, W., Craft, R.E., Ekstrom, M., Sexton, J., Sweetnam, J.: Data confidentiality: detect, respond to, and recover from data breaches (NIST special publication 1800–29). Technical report. SP 1800–29, National Institute of Standards and Technology (NIST)/National Cybersecurity Center of Excellence (NCCoE) (2024). https://nvlpubs.nist.gov/nistpubs/SpecialPublications/NIST.SP.1800-29.pdf. Accessed 13 Nov 2025
6. Initiative, J.T.F.T.: Guide for conducting risk assessments (special publication 800–30 revision 1). Technical report. SP 800–30 Rev 1, National Institute of Standards and Technology (NIST) (2012). https://nvlpubs.nist.gov/nistpubs/Legacy/SP/nistspecialpublication800-30r1.pdf. Accessed 13 Nov 2025
7. International Code of Conduct for Private Security Service Providers (ICoCA): Tool 3: Best practices for data storage. Technical report, International Code of Conduct for Private Security Service Providers (ICoCA) (2024). https://icoca.ch/wp-content/uploads/2024/11/Tool-3-Best-Practices-for-Data-Storage.pdf. Accessed 5 Nov 2025
8. Joint Task Force, N.I.o.S., Technology: Security and privacy controls for information systems and organizations. NIST Special Publication 800–34 Revision 1, National Institute of Standards and Technology (NIST) (2010)
9. Krogh, P.: Backup overview (2015). https://www.dpbestflow.org/backup/backup-overview#321. Accessed 13 Nov 2025
10. Le Monde: AWS, le service cloud d'Amazon, annonce avoir résolu la panne qui a touché des applications dans le monde entier (2025). https://www.lemonde.fr/pixels/article/2025/10/21/aws-le-service-cloud-d-amazon-annonce-avoir-resolu-la-panne-qui-a-touche-des-applications-dans-le-monde-entier_6648232_4408997.html. Accessed 13 Nov 2025
11. Le Monde: Microsoft Azure, deuxième plateforme cloud au monde, touchée par une panne (2025). https://www.lemonde.fr/pixels/article/2025/10/29/microsoft-azure-deuxieme-plateforme-cloud-au-monde-touche-par-une-panne_6650216_4408996.html. Accessed 13 Nov 2025
12. Levitin, G., Xing, L., Dai, Y.: Preventive replacements in real-time standby systems with periodic backups. IEEE Trans. Reliab. **66**(3), 771–782 (2017)
13. Levitin, G., Xing, L., Zhai, Q., Dai, Y.: Optimization of full versus incremental periodic backup policy. IEEE Trans. Dependable Secure Comput. **13**(6), 644–656 (2016)
14. Microsoft: Support matrix for backup with microsoft Azure backup server or system center DPM. Microsoft Learn (2025). https://learn.microsoft.com/en-us/azure/backup/backup-support-matrix-mabs-dpm. Accessed 15 Jan 2026

15. Morrison, R.: 3-2-1 vs 3-2-1-1 vs 3-2-1-1-0 backup rules. what is the difference between these strategies? (2024). https://www.baculasystems.com/blog/321-vs-3211-vs-32110-backup-rules/. Accessed 21 July 2024
16. Murphy, M.: Backup strategy. Linux J. **1996**(22es), 1-es (1996)
17. National Cybersecurity Center of Excellence: Protecting data from ransomware and other data loss events: a guide for managed service providers to conduct, maintain, and test backup files. NIST NCCoE Guide (2020). https://csrc.nist.gov/pubs/other/2020/04/24/protecting-data-from-ransomware-and-other-data-los/final, final
18. Nieles, M., Dempsey, K., Pillitteri, V.Y.: An introduction to information security. Special Publication 800–12 Revision 1 SP 800–12 Rev 1, National Institute of Standards and Technology (NIST) (2017). https://nvlpubs.nist.gov/nistpubs/SpecialPublications/NIST.SP.800-12r1.pdf. Accessed 13 Nov 2025
19. Panzarino, M.: How Pixar's Toy Story 2 was deleted twice, once by technology and again for its own good (2012). https://thenextweb.com/news/how-pixars-toy-story-2-was-deleted-twice-once-by-technology-and-again-for-its-own-good. Accessed 13 Nov 2025
20. Preston, W.C.: Lessons from the Dedoose disaster: why backing up your SaaS data is non-negotiable (2024). https://backupcentral.com/lessons-from-the-dedoose-disaster-why-backing-up-your-saas-data-is-non-negotiable/. Accessed 13 Nov 2025
21. RFI: Corée-du-sud : les archives gouvernementales sont parties en fumée, de très nombreuses données perdues (2025). https://www.rfi.fr/fr/asie-pacifique/20251010-cor%C3%A9e-du-sud-les-archives-gouvernementales-sont-parties-en-fum%C3%A9e-de-tr%C3%A8s-nombreuses-donn%C3%A9es-perdues. Accessed 13 Nov 2025
22. Romig, S.M.: Backup at ohio state, take 2. In: Proceedings of the Fourth Large Installation System Administrator's Conference (LISA IV)(USENIX Association: Berkeley, CA), p. 137 (1990)
23. Rydning, J., et al.: Worldwide global storagesphere forecast, 2021–2025: to save or not to save data, that is the question (2021). iDC Global StorageSphere Forecast, 2021–2025
24. Susnjara, S., Smalley, I.: What is data storage? IBM Think (2025). https://www.ibm.com/think/topics/data-storage?mhsrc=ibmsearch_a&mhq=data%20storage%20system. Accessed 17 Jan 2026
25. TechTarget: The 7 critical backup strategy best practices to keep data safe (2023). https://www.techtarget.com/searchdatabackup/feature/The-7-critical-backup-strategy-best-practices-to-keep-data-safe/. Accessed 13 Nov 2025
26. Venkatesan, V., Iliadis, I.: Effect of latent errors on the reliability of data storage systems. In: IEEE 21st International Symposium on Modelling, Analysis and Simulation of Computer and Telecommunication Systems, pp. 293–297 (2013)
27. Waldman, A.: Iowa hospital discloses breach following royal ransomware leak (2023). https://www.techtarget.com/searchsecurity/news/366538296/Iowa-hospital-discloses-breach-following-Royal-ransomware-leak. Accessed 15 Jan 2026

Heterogeneous Application Orchestration in Cyber-Physical Systems

Mehmet Cihan Sakman[1,4(✉)] , Valerio Schiavoni[1] , Ronny Seiger[2] ,
Olaf Zimmermann[3], and Josef Spillner[4]

[1] University of Neuchâtel, Neuchâtel, Switzerland
{mehmet.sakman,valerio.schiavoni}@unine.ch
[2] RWTH Aachen University, Aachen, Germany
ronny.seiger@rwth-aachen.de
[3] University of St. Gallen, St. Gallen, Switzerland
olaf.zimmermann@unisg.ch
[4] ZHAW, Winterthur, Switzerland
josef.spillner@zhaw.ch

Abstract. Cyber-physical systems (CPS) operate across a computing
continuum of heterogeneous devices with varying support for execution
formats such as containers, Wasm, and native binaries. While Kubernetes
is the de facto orchestration standard, its container-centric model and
operational overhead make it unsuitable for resource-constrained embedded devices in CPS deployments. We present an adaptive orchestration
system that treats format heterogeneity as a first-class concern, enabling
distributed deployment across heterogeneous CPS environments. The
system selects and places components based on device capabilities and
user-specified non-functional requirements (NFRs). Through a MAPE-K
control loop, local device agents continuously monitor and report constraints to a central orchestrator. Upon detecting a constraint violation,
the orchestrator directs the agents to locally adapt through execution
format transformations, redeployments, or component suspensions. Evaluation on a distributed image processing pipeline of five microservices
demonstrates deployment initialization in $< 5\,\mathrm{min}$, rapid execution format transformation in $< 3\,\mathrm{s}$, and a stable agent memory footprint of
30–40 MB even under active load. These results establish that dynamic,
NFR-driven heterogeneous orchestration can be achieved with minimal
overhead in resource-constrained CPS environments.

1 Introduction

Cyber-physical systems rely on a computing continuum that spans data cen-
tres, edge gateways, and resource-constrained devices deployed at the physical
edge [30]. This architectural diversity reflects the distributed nature of CPS:
sensor fusion occurs near data sources to reduce latency, control loops require
proximity to actuators, and high-throughput analytics builds on cloud scalability [31]. Controlling this multi-tier reality in software is challenging, as common
orchestration paradigms assume a level of resource homogeneity absent in CPS.

© IFIP International Federation for Information Processing 2026
Published by Springer Nature Switzerland AG 2026
A. Nunes Alonso and R. Palmieri (Eds.): DAIS 2026, LNCS 16591, pp. 72–88, 2026.
https://doi.org/10.1007/978-3-032-27358-1_5

Kubernetes has become the dominant orchestration framework, including in cyber-physical and edge-oriented deployments [7,25]. However, Kubernetes is fundamentally designed for relatively homogeneous clusters with stable resource availability and a uniform container runtime model [34,39]. CPS violate these assumptions along two critical dimensions. First, resource-constrained and embedded devices often lack the memory, CPU capacity, or operating system support required to efficiently host container runtimes and the Kubernetes node stack [20]. Second, CPS deployments operate under strict non-functional requirements (NFRs) that extend beyond performance metrics, including energy budgets on battery-powered devices, thermal constraints on passively cooled nodes, fuel levels and availability guarantees for safety-critical or remote components [11]. While Kubernetes supports basic resource limits and node affinity, it lacks support for sustainability constraints such as preferring devices with stable power supplies, avoiding overheating on passively-cooled devices, and prioritizing critical workloads during resource shortages [24].

In response, developers often adopt a pragmatic workaround: deploy all components as containers on a single host, effectively using Kubernetes within its intended homogeneous, resource-stable operating model. This centralised approach is operationally simple but forfeits benefits such as distributed computing, reduced network traffic, increased fault tolerance, and reduced total energy consumption with heterogeneous power profiles. The irony is that devices best suited for sustainable operation (solar-powered edge devices) are underutilised because orchestration tools struggle to reason about non-functional constraints such as energy availability, thermal limits, or intermittent connectivity [24,26].

The core obstacle is the combination of execution-format homogeneity and limited awareness of non-functional constraints in current orchestration systems. Many constrained devices can execute lightweight workloads when appropriate formats are used. Wasm runtimes, for example, are designed for fast startup and low memory footprints, making them suitable for environments where container-based execution is impractical [14,21]. Similarly, native binaries can be deployed on capable nodes to avoid runtime overhead. Both execution formats and device-level constraints are well understood; what is missing is an orchestration layer that treats execution-format heterogeneity and NFRs as first-class concerns.

Moreover, CPS environments are inherently dynamic. Energy availability, thermal conditions, device health, and workload characteristics evolve over time, invalidating static placement decisions made at deployment. Effective CPS orchestration therefore requires continuous monitoring and constraint-aware adaptation, allowing workloads to be redistributed or execution formats adjusted as devices approach operational limits. Such feedback-driven control aligns with established autonomic management models like MAPE-K loops [18].

To align with these concerns, this paper makes the following contributions:

- An NFR-driven adaptive orchestration framework for heterogeneous CPS environments, where device capabilities, sustainability-related NFRs, and runtime format support are jointly considered during distributed deployment.
- A runtime-adaptive orchestration system that performs constraint-aware component placement and reconfiguration using MAPE-K control loops to maintain system stability.

– A semi-automated Wasm component builder that bridges the gap between stateful Python development and stateless Wasm execution. This tool automates the extraction and compilation of computational logic into Wasm binaries, eliminating the need for manual refactoring.
– Demonstration of the system on a heterogeneous edge-to-cloud testbed running a distributed image processing pipeline. Our evaluation confirms that NFR-driven adaptation—specifically dynamic format switching—reduces artefact storage overhead by up to 75% and enables sub-3-second reconfiguration latencies under constraint violations.

The paper is structured as follows: Sect. 2 provides background on CPS environments, orchestration limitations, relevant execution formats, and NFRs. Section 3 discusses related work. Section 4 details our system design and architecturally significant requirements. Section 5 describes the prototype implementation, followed by the experimental evaluation in Sect. 6. Section 7 summarizes and concludes.

2   Background

To contextualize the need for adaptive orchestration, this section outlines the CPS computing continuum, the limitations of container-centric approaches, and the dynamic NFRs that necessitate heterogeneous execution formats.

2.1   The CPS Computing Continuum

CPS span a continuum from cloud infrastructure to resource-constrained IoT devices. The heterogeneous layering reflects physical reality: sensors co-located with monitored processes, edge nodes enabling low-latency control loops, cloud resources providing scalable analytics. Cloud nodes provide multi-core x86_64 processors with tens of gigabytes of memory, edge gateways use ARM SoCs with 1–4 GB RAM, and embedded devices have 256–512 MB memory with single-core CPUs clocked at hundreds of MHz. Power profiles range from stable data center supplies to battery power and energy harvesting. Network connectivity spans high-bandwidth wired connections to constrained wireless protocols.

2.2   Kubernetes and the Homogeneity Assumption

Kubernetes abstracts infrastructure as clusters of nodes capable of executing containerized workloads under a unified control plane. This abstraction works well in homogeneous servers. When extended to CPS, it exposes several fundamental mismatches between Kubernetes' design assumptions and CPS realities.

Resource Requirements. Its node agent (kubelet) maintains continuous communication with the control plane and manages container lifecycles, requiring a nontrivial resource footprint [39]. While lightweight Kubernetes distributions such as K3s or K0s reduce control-plane binary size and initial memory requirements, the operational overhead remains significant on many edge-deployed devices [37].

In addition, container runtimes introduce further memory and storage overhead through image management, background daemons, and filesystem layers. On constrained devices, this baseline consumption significantly reduces the capacity available for application workloads, limiting deployment feasibility.

Container Runtime Overhead. Containers obtain namespaced isolation through cgroups, assuming a fully-featured Linux kernel. While efforts such as K3s and KubeEdge [1] reduce the footprint, they cannot eliminate the fundamental runtime overhead with layering, union filesystems, and daemon processes [39].

Operational Complexity. Kubernetes assumes reliable connectivity, sufficient storage for images, and rolling update capability. Embedded devices lack these requirements. These are not flaws but consequences of design choices optimized for Kubernetes' primary use case which is a subset of the CPS continuum.

2.3   Heterogeneous Execution Formats

CPS require support for multiple execution formats to accommodate device diversity. We identify three format classes. *Containers* provide process isolation through OS-level virtualization, mature tooling and vast ecosystems. Implementations include Docker, Podman, and LXC [4]. Despite overhead, containers remain the preferred choice for servers and capable edge gateways with sufficient memory and storage. *WebAssembly (Wasm)* serves as lightweight, portable alternative. Runtimes like WasmEdge [36] and Wasmtime [6] require minimal memory (often $< 50\,\mathrm{MB}$), start in milliseconds, and provide sandboxing without OS support [13,22,38], making them suitable for constrained devices where containers exceed resources. However, the Wasm ecosystem is less mature. *Native execution* directly on the host OS eliminates the overhead and simplifies hardware access, though it sacrifices portability and isolation.

These execution formats are *complementary*, not competitive. A single CPS application might appropriately use containers on edge gateways, Wasm on moderately constrained sensors, and native binaries on specialized microcontrollers. Current orchestration frameworks, however, assume format homogeneity and lack mechanisms to reason about format-specific constraints.

2.4   Non-Functional Requirements (NFRs) and Constraints in CPS

CPS deployments must satisfy operational constraints beyond functional correctness. We identify critical NFR dimensions following the ISO/IEC 25010 quality model [15], extended with sustainability as a distinct category following the Karlskrona Manifesto's principles for environmental and economic considerations [3].

Energy Efficiency and Sustainability. Battery-powered or energy-harvesting devices operate within explicit power budgets. Solar-powered nodes must adapt workloads to energy availability; violating constraints risks device shutdown or reduced operational lifetime. Energy efficiency has emerged as a prominent sustainability concern in distributed systems [2,27,32], yet existing orchestration approaches operate within single execution formats and do not consider format heterogeneity as an adaptation mechanism.

Thermal Constraints. Passively-cooled sensors have maximum operating temperatures where compute-intensive workloads can cause overheating, leading to throttling, errors, or hardware damage. Thermal management is a physical constraint that must be actively monitored and enforced through orchestration.

Criticality and Availability. Applications have varying criticality levels: control loops governing physical safety must maintain continuous operation (high availability), while monitoring or logging services can tolerate degradation during resource contention. This criticality-based prioritization aligns with reliability requirements in safety-critical CPS.

These constraints are inherently dynamic: energy availability fluctuates, ambient temperature affects thermal capacity, and workloads shift unpredictably. Kubernetes alone provides CPU and memory limits and basic placement controls, but cannot react to thermal stress, adapt to renewable energy cycles, or suspend lower-priority workloads when critical services require resources. NFR satisfaction can benefit from execution formats: a service violating thermal or energy constraints, as a container may operate within limits as a Wasm module, enabling deployment where container execution would be infeasible.

3   Related Work

Container and Edge Orchestration. Kubernetes and its lightweight and edge variants such as K3s and KubeEdge provide mature container orchestration with custom-metric scheduling and partial NFR-aware placement [33,39]. However, these systems primarily optimize placement decisions within a container-centric control plane and rely on static packaging assumptions. Hybrid edge designs such as [17] explore hybrid virtualization (combining containers and unikernels) to improve resource utilization on constrained IoT nodes. Their evaluation, however, is restricted to specific hardware classes and focuses on design-time architectural trade-offs rather than continuous runtime adaptation. Likewise, autonomous energy-aware schedulers for serverless edge computing [2,32] employ MAPE-K control loops to monitor battery-powered nodes, yet dynamically offload tasks based on energy availability zones, without considering execution format transition or runtime optimization

Declarative Modeling and TOSCA-Based Approaches. TOSCA [23] enables declarative specification of application topologies and NFRs. Platforms such as OpenTOSCA [5] and Cloudify [8] support automated deployment and policy-driven orchestration, including extensions for edge and IoT scenarios. These approaches emphasize model-driven provisioning and constraint-aware placement but typically operate at deployment time, with limited support for closed-loop adaptation. Furthermore, policy enforcement is usually limited to placement and scaling decisions, without integrating dynamic execution-environment management.

WebAssembly in Distributed and Serverless Systems. Systems such as wasm-Cloud [35] and Fermyon [12] enable distributed Wasm deployment, while Krustlet [10] integrates WASI workloads into Kubernetes by replacing the kubelet and executing modules without relying on a traditional container runtime. However, the Krustlet project is no longer actively maintained and has largely been superseded by containerd-based approaches such as runwasi [9], which embed Wasm runtimes as shims within containerd to allow coexistence with containers under a unified control plane. Authors in [19] explore Wasm-native orchestration as an extension to Kubernetes, demonstrating Wasm as a portable and efficient execution substrate while remaining tied to container-centric or serverless control planes. In contrast, we treat Wasm and native binaries as first-class orchestration targets that can bypass container runtimes entirely, reducing per-node footprint and runtime overhead. Additionally, we support automated transformation from source components to executable Wasm artifacts, facilitating seamless adoption of lightweight execution formats in heterogeneous edge deployments.

4   System Design

This section details the architecture and operational mechanics of the proposed orchestration framework, progressing from core design objectives to system components, declarative configuration, and the runtime adaptation loop.

4.1   Design Objectives

Addressing the architectural limitations and CPS requirements outlined in Sect. 2.1, we derive four Architecturally Significant Requirements (ASRs):

- **R1: Heterogeneity Support.** The system must support multiple execution formats (Containers, Wasm, Native) rather than assuming a uniform runtime.
- **R2: Minimal Orchestration Overhead.** The agents must operate within strict embedded resource limits (e.g., $<50\,\mathrm{MB}$ idle memory) to maximize capacity for application workloads.
- **R3: NFR-Driven Adaptation.** The system must evaluate and react to physical constraints (e.g., energy, thermal) beyond standard computational limits (CPU/RAM).
- **R4: Dynamic Lifecycle Management.** The system must continuously react to sensor measurements and adapt system state to ensure workloads remain active and available.

To fulfill these ASRs, our autonomic orchestration framework employs a MAPE-K control loop to manage multi-format execution (Container, Wasm, Native) alongside dynamic service placement and lifecycle management in heterogeneous CPS environments.

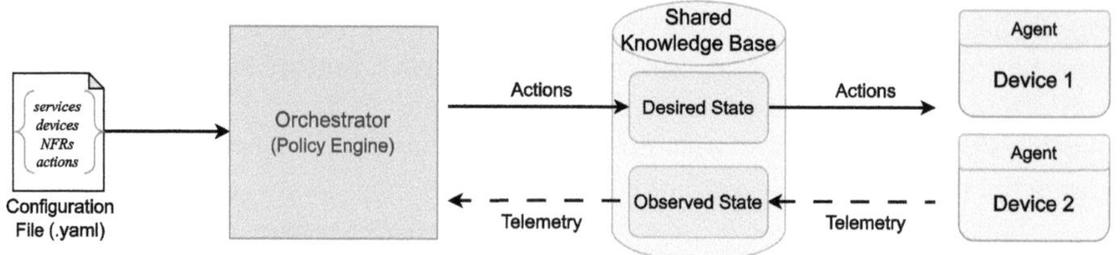

Fig. 1. Conceptual architecture of the NFR-driven orchestration system.

4.2   Architecture Overview

The system comprises three components (cf. Fig. 1): a central orchestrator, agents, and a shared knowledge base. While the implementation focuses on Containers, Wasm, and Native processes, the architectural separation between planning and enactment allows additional execution backends to be integrated through agent-side runtime adapters. The orchestrator reads deployment specifications, evaluates constraint rules, and issues adaptation commands. Agents monitor and report local resources, and execute deployment actions. The shared knowledge base serves as the coordination backbone and implements the Knowledge (K) component of the MAPE-K loop. It maintains two abstract views: an *observed state* reflecting telemetry from agents and a *desired state* representing deployment rules and adaptation decisions computed by the orchestrator.

Users specify deployments via a YAML configuration defining services (multi-format microservices), devices (resource profiles and supported formats), constraints (operational thresholds), and actions (rule-based policies). The orchestrator prepares all required artifacts, multi-architecture container images and Wasm components, before deployment, distributing them to registered devices. This pre-deployment phase eliminates transfer delays at runtime.

Communication is database-centric for simplicity, though the architecture supports alternative coordination mechanisms (e.g., message queues or REST APIs). Agents poll the database for commands and write status updates, while the orchestrator evaluates observed state and issues adaptation directives.

4.3   Configuration Model

Deployment specifications follow a declarative model capturing devices, services, constraints, and adaptation policies as depicted in Fig. 2. Constraint thresholds are expressed as percentages (CPU $\mathbb{C}$, memory $\mathbb{M}$ & battery $\mathbb{B}$ utilization) or absolute values (temperature, power consumption, network latency). These constraints span multiple NFR dimensions: $\mathbb{C}$ and $\mathbb{M}$ utilization reflect performance efficiency, $\mathbb{B}$ and power consumption address energy sustainability, and temperature represents thermal management for passively-cooled embedded devices where sustained computation can cause overheating and hardware damage. The system supports three adaptation actions: MIGRATE relocates services to different devices maintaining format where supported, TRANSFORM switches exe-

```
devices:
  - name: edge
    cpu_cores: 4
    memory_mb: 4096
    formats: [container, wasm]
    static_ip: 10.10.100.1
    platform: linux/arm64
  - name: sensor
    cpu_cores: 1
    memory_mb: 512
    formats: [wasm, native]
    static_ip: 10.20.100.1
    platform: linux/arm64
  - name: cloud
    cpu_cores: 16
    memory_mb: 32768
    formats: [container]
    static_ip: 192.168.1.100
    platform: linux/amd64
```

```
services:
  - name: image-preprocessor
    preferred: [sensor,edge,cloud]
    formats:
      container:
        image: repo/preprocessor
        build: ./services/pre
      wasm:
        wit: ./pre/interface.wit
        impl: ./services/pre/worker.py
    constraints:
      cpu:
        critical: 90.0
        medium: 70.0
        healthy: 50.0
    actions:
      cpu:
        medium: [TRANSFORM]
        critical: [MIGRATE]
```

(a) Device profiles defining resources.   (b) Service constraints and formats.

Fig. 2. View of the unified `configuration.yaml` file presenting device profiles (a) and service specifications (b).

cution format on the same device (container $\leftrightarrow$ Wasm), and PAUSE suspends non-critical services. The `preferred` list defines initial placement order; future work will incorporate intelligent device selection.

4.4 MAPE-K Control Loop and Adaptation

The system implements a MAPE-K control loop [18] for heterogeneous runtime orchestration (cf. Fig. 3) addressing dynamic lifecycle management (R4). Agents continuously `Monitor` resource metrics ($\mathbb{C}$, $\mathbb{M}$, $\mathbb{B}$, temperature) at configurable intervals, writing measurements to the shared database (`Knowledge`). The orchestrator polls for agent reports, `Analyzing` metrics against declarative constraint thresholds and violation persistence conditions. Violations trigger adaptation `Planning`: the orchestrator identifies affected services, evaluates permitted actions, and selects candidate devices for migration or format transformation. MIGRATE relocates a service to a different device from the `preferred` list that satisfies constraints and supports the service's format; if the target supports only a different format, migration implicitly includes transformation. TRANSFORM switches execution format on the same device (e.g., container $\rightarrow$ Wasm to reduce memory footprint), requiring brief service interruption. PAUSE suspends execution when neither migration nor transformation can satisfy constraints; if no valid action succeeds, the orchestrator logs a warning and stops the service to protect devices. When multiple actions are applicable for the same violation, the orchestrator resolves them according to the left-to-right priority order defined in the configuration, ensuring deterministic adaptation and preventing conflicting enactment requests for the same service.

Agents poll the database for commands and `Execute` locally: managing service lifecycles and format switches. The shared database maintains system state across device capabilities (*devices*), service deployments (*services*), constraints (*constraints*), and adaptation history (*actions*). Agent heartbeats enable failure detection; missing updates trigger device offline status and service migration. To prevent thrashing and overreaction to transient spikes, the system implements hysteresis: constraints must remain violated for a configurable number of consecutive monitoring cycles before triggering adaptation, and cooldown periods prevent rapid re-adaptation after enactment. When constraints return to `healthy` ranges, the orchestrator restores the initial service placement defined in `preferred`, ensuring a predictable deployment topology.

4.5 Multi-Format Artifact Management

To satisfy the format heterogeneity (`R1`), the orchestrator prepares execution artifacts for all currently supported service formats defined in the configuration before deployment. For containers, Buildx generates multi-architecture images supporting x86_64 and ARM platforms, ensuring compatibility across the device continuum. For Wasm, the system automates component generation from Python source code.

The Wasm build pipeline extracts pure computational logic from standard Python workers using static analysis to remove database connections, networking code, and control loops. The extracted logic is wrapped in a Component Model v2 adapter matching the service's `.wit` interface definition. The adapter is then compiled using `componentize-py` and executed via `Wasmtime`. This automation currently supports services with cleanly structured code separating business logic from infrastructure concerns; future work will extend to additional languages and handle more complex code patterns for the Wasm format.

During the deployment initialization phase, pre-built artifacts are distributed to all candidate devices listed in `preferred`. Agents store artifacts locally, enabling sub-second format switching during `TRANSFORM` operations without network transfer overhead. Native execution, when specified, are assumed user-provided and deployed similarly.

5 Implementation

This section details our open-source implementation [28]. Figure 3 illustrates the end-to-end operational pipeline, capturing both artifact provisioning and runtime coordination between the central orchestrator and distributed agents.

5.1 System Components

The orchestrator executes on a designated coordination host with access to a shared SQL database and a local container registry (code available [28]). Upon boot, the orchestrator parses the `configuration.yaml` manifest to extract service definitions, device capability profiles, supported execution formats, placement preferences, and constraint policies. Based on the declared formats, it first builds all required multi-arch container images and populates the local registry.

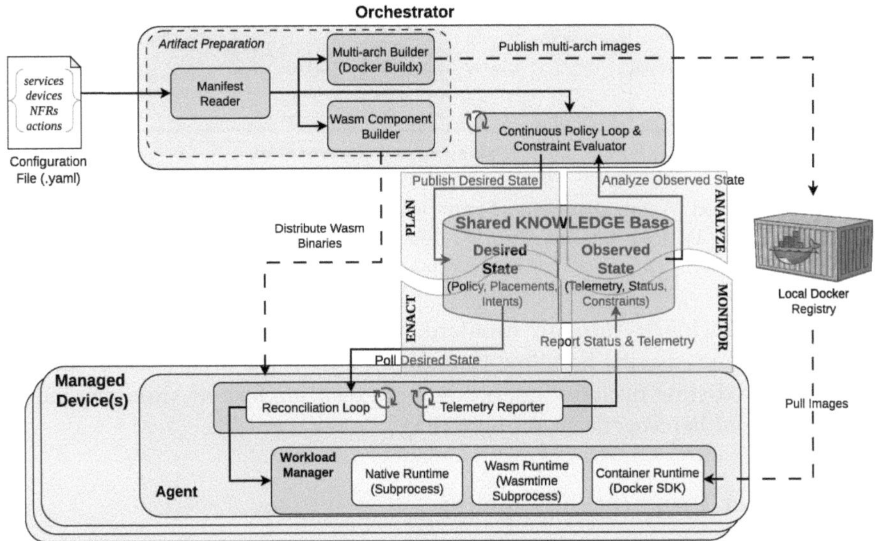

Fig. 3. System architecture implementing the MAPE-K cycle. The `Orchestrator` handles the *Analyze & Plan* phases alongside artifact preparation. The `Knowledge Base` synchronizes state with `Devices`, where `Agents` perform *Enact* (reconciliation) & *Monitor* (telemetry) operations.

If any candidate device supports Wasm execution, a dedicated automation utility compiles the corresponding service implementations into portable Wasm component binaries and distributes them to the supported devices.

After artifact preparation, the orchestrator computes initial service-to-device assignments based on placement priorities and capabilities, writing them to the shared database as the desired state. It then transitions into continuous analysis mode. The constraint evaluator parses NFRs as thresholds and adaptation actions. Orchestrator evaluates these against the observed state and updates the desired state, fulfilling the requirement for NFR-driven adaptation (R3).

Agents run as containers on each managed device. Each agent includes a telemetry reporter that periodically measures abstract device state and writes it to the shared database as observed state. The agent's primary reconciliation loop polls the desired state and manages the local service lifecycle accordingly. The agent container exhibits an idle memory footprint of approximately 30–40 MB, excluding managed services, satisfying the requirement for minimal orchestration overhead (R2). Execution format management varies by runtime but remains encapsulated within the agent. For container-based services, agents use the Docker Python SDK to pull images from the local registry, create or terminate containers, and inspect runtime status. For Wasm services, agents launch the Wasmtime runtime as a subprocess, execute the compiled component binary, and manage it via process control mechanisms. For native execution, agents spawn the executable directly as a subprocess with appropriate environment

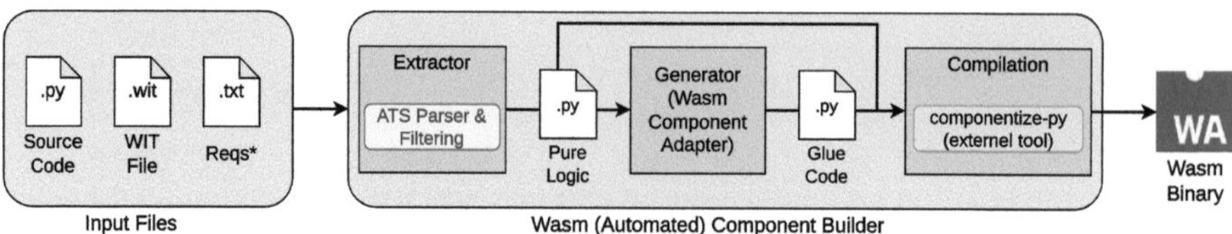

Fig. 4. Automated Wasm component generation pipeline illustrating logic extraction and artifact compilation. The asterisk (*) denotes optional inputs.

variables, managing it through standard process signals without intermediary runtimes. Format-specific handling is abstracted from the orchestrator, allowing uniform desired-state updates independent of execution format, directly realizing the objective of heterogeneity support (**R1**).

5.2   Artifact Preparation Pipeline

Orchestration begins with *artifact preparation*, a pre-deployment phase transforming configurations into deployable executables. This decouples building from the runtime lifecycle, ensuring artifacts (container images, Wasm and native binaries) are locally available on candidate devices to eliminate network overhead during adaptation.

Multi-architecture container images are generated by the *Multi-arch Builder* (cf. Fig. 3). The orchestrator parses the manifest for target architectures (e.g., `linux/amd64`, `linux/arm64`) and uses Buildx to build variants in parallel. These are pushed to the local registry, enabling agents to pull hardware-specific images without on-device compilation.

Semi-Automated Wasm component builder operationalize the Python logic in restricted environment (cf. Fig. 4). This pipeline addresses a fundamental architectural mismatch: while developers rely on stateful services with direct database access, Wasm components are often treated as stateless in practice due to the immaturity of the ecosystem—specifically, the WASI-SQL interface remains a stagnant Phase 1 proposal [16]. To mitigate the need for manual refactoring, our pipeline automates the transformation of Python workers into compliant, stateless artifacts. The process executes within a reproducible Docker-based factory. First, an *extractor* parses the WebAssembly Interface Types (`.wit`) and performs static analysis to selectively isolate pure computational logic, discarding unsupported infrastructure code like database loops. Second, a *generator* synthesizes a Component Model adapter to bridge Python's dynamic typing with Wasm's strict interfaces. Finally, the *compilation* step runs `componentize-py` to bundle the interpreter and dependencies into a standalone binary, effectively decoupling the developer's logic from the complexities of the Wasm toolchain.

Currently, Wasm/WASI components have limited support for native Python extensions [29], requiring developers to structure implementations using pure

Table 1. Testbed device specifications and supported execution formats.

Device	Model	CPU	Memory	Platform	Formats
PC	Core Ultra 5 135U	12 cores	32768 MB	linux/amd64	C, W, N
Edge	Raspberry Pi 400	4 cores	4096 MB	linux/arm64	C, W, N
NAS	QNAP TS-216G	4 cores	4096 MB	linux/arm64	C, N

C = Container,   W = WebAssembly,   N = Native

Python libraries compatible with the target Wasm runtime. Furthermore, function names in the source code must match the exports declared in the .wit interface for the *extractor* to identify valid entry points. Since components are invoked per request in our deployment model, developers must provide a host wrapper script to manage the service's control loop (e.g., database polling), which the orchestrator launches to trigger the Wasm component at runtime.

Resulting Wasm binaries range from 20–40 MB, significantly smaller than equivalent 100–150 MB container images. This reduction benefits constrained storage and accelerates adaptation: switching formats requires only starting a new subprocess rather than unpacking image layers.

6   Evaluation

We evaluate the NFR-driven adaptive orchestration system using a distributed image processing pipeline deployed across heterogeneous CPS infrastructure. This evaluation assesses whether the system satisfies the design objectives (R1-R4) in Sect. 4.1 by measuring initialization overhead, multi-format artifact footprint, and operational behavior under NFR-driven reconfiguration.

6.1   Experimental Setup

Testbed. We deploy a YOLOv8-based distributed image processing pipeline across three heterogeneous devices (edge-to-cloud) to validate our design objectives (Sect. 4.1). Its computational intensity induces the physical constraints (CPU, power) needed to evaluate NFR-driven adaptation (R3) and lifecycle management (R4). Furthermore, the architectural diversity (x86_64 and ARM64) demonstrates format heterogeneity (R1) and proves the agent operates with minimal overhead on constrained nodes (R2).

Table 1 summarizes the device specifications. All devices share access to the database hosted on the PC and network-attached storage (NAS) via NFS mounts. The PC hosts the orchestrator and a local container registry. Each device, including the PC, runs an agent that reconciles desired state and manages the local service lifecycle.

Workload and Policies. The pipeline consists of five microservices: **ingest** registers incoming data; **preprocess** normalizes images; **analyze_light** performs

Table 2. Service deployments and threshold-based adaptation policies.

Service	Preference	Fmt	Constraint (H / M / Cr)	Actions
`ingest`	PC	C	—	—
`preprocess`	PC	C	—	—
`analyze_light`	Edge, PC	C, W	CPU: 50/70/90%	M:TR, Cr:MG
`analyze_heavy`	Edge, PC	C	Pwr: 80/–/20%	Cr:MG
`store_index`	NAS	C	Mem: 50/–/90%	Cr:PS

H / M / Cr = Healthy / Medium / Critical thresholds.   C = Container,
W = WebAssembly.   TR = Transform,   MG = Migrate,   PS = Pause.

Table 3. Service artifact sizes (Wasm only where supported).

	ingest	preprocess	analyze_light	analyze_heavy	store_index
Container	184 MB	164 MB	164 MB	1870 MB	175 MB
Wasm	—	—	39 MB	—	—

lightweight filtering; `analyze_heavy` executes YOLOv8 object detection; and
`store_index` persists results. Table 2 details the initial placement preferences,
execution formats, and constraint-driven adaptation policies for each service. To
prevent oscillation, orchestrator enforces a 3-cycle (30 s) violation persistence
check before triggering adaptation, followed by a 60 s cooldown.

Artifact Sizes. Table 3 reports the uncompressed artifact sizes. Container images
are stored and transferred as compressed layer archives by the local registry;
consequently, the data pulled over the network is substantially smaller than
the reported uncompressed size. Layers already cached on a device are skipped
entirely, further reducing pull latency for subsequent deployments. Despite
bundling YOLOv8n model weights, agents pulled the `analyze_heavy` image in
under 100 s. For `analyze_light`, the 39 MB Wasm module represents over 75%
size reduction compared to its 164 MB container counterpart, enabling rapid
format switching on edge nodes.

6.2   Results

System Initialization. Full pipeline deployment completed in under five minutes from orchestrator boot to all five services reaching a running state across
the three devices. As reported in Table 3, artifact sizes vary considerably: most
pipeline stages occupy 164–184 MB as container images, while `analyze_heavy`
reaches 1.87 GB owing to its bundled model weights. Despite this, the heaviest
image was pulled over the local network in approximately 70 s, with all necessary artifacts across the pipeline retrieved in under 100 s. During this phase, the
agents maintained a stable memory footprint of 30–40 MB even while parsing
desired state, coordinating multi-format artifact downloads, and continuously

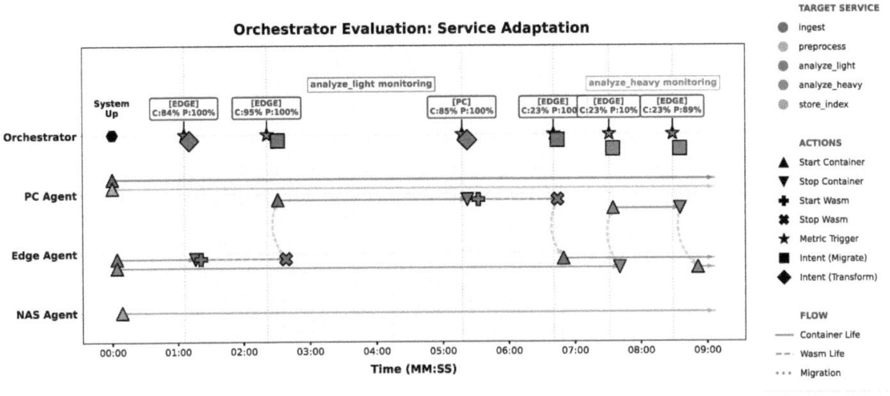

Fig. 5. Timeline of orchestration events showing service lifecycle actions, intent triggers, and telemetry-driven adaptations.

reporting telemetry. This consistent resource profile confirms adherence to the minimal orchestration overhead requirement (R2) under idle and active load.

Manual Triggering and Timing Interpretation. To evaluate adaptation behavior in a controlled and reproducible manner, constraint violations were triggered manually rather than relying on organic workload-driven telemetry from the agents and represented by a star in Fig. 5. This approach decouples adaptation mechanics from workload variability and enables precise observation of system response under known, repeatable conditions. Accordingly, all reaction times reported below reflect the orchestrator's adaptation loop latency and the time required for services to reach an operational state where they can accept work; they do not include application-level cold-start overhead such as model loading or initialization of service-specific resources.

NFR/Constraint-Driven Adaptation. Figure 5 presents the orchestration timeline, visualizing service execution flows and migration paths alongside lifecycle events, metric triggers, and issued intents. Two services undergo constraint-driven adaptation: `analyze_light` due to CPU pressure, and `analyze_heavy` due to power depletion.

For `analyze_light`, the orchestrator records a CPU utilization ($\mathbb{C}$) of 84% on the Edge device, exceeding the 70% medium threshold defined in Table 2. After three consecutive monitoring cycles confirm the sustained violation (approximately 30 s), the orchestrator issues a TRANSFORM intent, instructing the Edge agent to replace the running container with a Wasm process on the same host. The end-to-end transition completes in 3 s, demonstrating rapid NFR-driven adaptation (R3) via format transformation (R1). When $\mathbb{C}$ subsequently spikes to 95%, exceeding the 90% critical threshold, the orchestrator escalates to a MIGRATE intent, relocating `analyze_light` to the PC. There, $\mathbb{C}$ rises to 85%, again exceeding the threshold, triggering another TRANSFORM intent that converts the service from container to Wasm on the PC. Once the Edge device returns to a healthy state after the 60-second cooldown, the orchestrator migrates `analyze_light` back to Edge and restores its original container format, re-establishing the initial deployment configuration via continuous lifecycle management (R4). This demonstrates the system's ability to not only react to constraint violations across devices but also to restore services to their preferred placement once conditions stabilize.

For `analyze_heavy`, a power depletion on the Edge device–battery level ($\mathbb{B}$) falling below the 20% critical threshold in Table 2–triggers a MIGRATE intent. The orchestrator moves the container to the PC. When $\mathbb{B}$ recovers to 89% and stabilizes above the healthy threshold after the 60-s cooldown, the orchestrator migrates `analyze_heavy` back to its original Edge placement, demonstrating successful constraint resolution and service restoration to the preferred deployment configuration.

7 Conclusion

We contribute an adaptive, NFR-driven orchestration framework that treats execution format heterogeneity and physical constraints (e.g., energy, thermal limits) as first-class concerns to overcome the limitations of traditional, container-centric CPS deployments. By implementing a MAPE-K control loop, the system continuously monitors device states and dynamically manages service lifecycles through in-place format transformations, component migrations, or suspensions [28]. Our evaluation on a distributed edge-to-cloud image processing pipeline successfully validated our architecturally significant requirements (R1-R4). Specifically, full system deployment–encompassing multi-architecture artifact preparation, distribution, and initial agent bootstrapping–completed in under five minutes, successfully handling complex model artifacts up to 1.87 GB. Furthermore, constraint-driven format switching between container and Web-Assembly runtimes executed in under 3 s, resolving critical resource pressure locally without requiring network-intensive migrations. Throughout these active lifecycle events, agents maintained a highly stable 30–40 MB memory footprint. These results demonstrate that dynamic, multi-format orchestration can be achieved with minimal overhead, preserving essential compute capacity on resource-constrained edge nodes. Future work will explore alternative coordination mechanisms to improve scalability; extend the agent-based architecture to support additional execution backends beyond containers, Wasm, and native processes; integrate learning-based policy engines for adaptive constraint synthesis; and broaden Wasm automation beyond Python to increase CPS applicability.

Acknowledgments. This work has received funding from the Swiss National Science Foundation under Grant No. 10002384 (*TaSSAreCt* project).

References

1. Kubernetes Native Edge Computing. https://kubeedge.io/. Accessed 19 Feb 2026
2. Aslanpour, M.S., Toosi, A.N., Cheema, M.A., Gaire, R.: Energy-aware resource scheduling for serverless edge computing. In: 2022 22nd IEEE International Symposium on Cluster, Cloud and Internet Computing (CCGrid), pp. 190–199 (2022)
3. Becker, C., Chitchyan, R., Duboc, L.: Sustainability design and software: the Karlskrona manifesto. In: IEEE/ACM 37th IEEE International Conference on Software Engineering, vol. 2, pp. 467–476 (2015)
4. Ben Kebaier, N., Geib, B., Lyczkowski, E., Venanzi, R., Barth, M.: Real-time performance evaluation of containerized virtual PLCs: a comparative study of docker and podman for industrial automation. In: IEEE 30th Intl Workshop on Computer Aided Modeling and Design (CAMAD), pp. 1–6 (2025)
5. Binz, T., Breitenbücher, U., Haupt, F.: OpenTOSCA - a runtime for TOSCA-based cloud applications. In: Basu, S., Pautasso, C., Zhang, L., Fu, X. (eds.) Service-Oriented Computing. ICSOC 2013. LNCS, vol. 8274, pp. 692–695. Springer, Berlin, Heidelberg (2013). https://doi.org/10.1007/978-3-642-45005-1_62
6. Bytecode Alliance: Wasmtime: A lightweight WebAssembly runtime (2025). https://wasmtime.dev. Accessed 14 Aug 2025
7. Cai, Z., Buyya, R.: Inverse queuing model-based feedback control for elastic container provisioning of web systems in Kubernetes. IEEE Trans. Comput. **71**(2), 337–348 (2022)
8. Cloudify Platform Ltd.: Cloudify: Open Source TOSCA-based Cloud Orchestration Platform (2024). https://docs.cloudify.co/. Accessed 16 Feb 2026
9. containerd Project: runwasi: WebAssembly Shim for containerd (2023). https://github.com/containerd/runwasi. Accessed 16 Feb 2026
10. deislabs: Krustlet: Kubernetes Kubelet for WebAssembly (2020). https://github.com/krustlet/krustlet. Accessed 16 Feb 2026
11. Derler, P., Lee, E.A., Sangiovanni Vincentelli, A.: Modeling cyber-physical systems. Proc. IEEE **100**(1), 13–28 (2012)
12. Fermyon Technologies: Spin: Developer Tool for Building WebAssembly Microservices (2021). https://developer.fermyon.com/spin/. Accessed 16 Feb 2026
13. Haas, A., Rossberg, A., Schuff, D.L.: Bringing the web up to speed with WebAssembly. In: Proceedings of the 38th ACM SIGPLAN Conference on Programming Language Design and Implementation, pp. 185–200 (2017)
14. Has, M., Xiong, T., Abdesslem, F.B., Kušek, M.: WebAssembly on Resource-Constrained IoT Devices: Performance, Efficiency, and Portability (2025). https://arxiv.org/abs/2512.00035
15. ISO/IEC: ISO/IEC 25010:2011 Systems and software engineering Product quality model. International Organization for Standardization (2011). https://www.iso.org/standard/35733.html
16. Zhou, J., Dan Chiarlone, D.J.: WebAssembly System Interface, SQL API (2024). https://github.com/WebAssembly/wasi-sql. Accessed 16 Feb 2026
17. Kaiser, S., Tosun, A.S., Korkmaz, T.: Edge System Design Using Containers and Unikernels for IoT Applications (2024). https://arxiv.org/abs/2412.03032
18. Kephart, J., Chess, D.: The vision of autonomic computing. Computer **36**, 41–50 (2003)
19. Kjorveziroski, V., Filiposka, S.: WebAssembly orchestration in the context of serverless computing. J. Netw. Syst. Manag. **31** (2023)

20. Kodakandla, N.: Optimizing Kubernetes for edge computing: challenges and innovative. Solutions **4**, 210–221 (2021)
21. Ménétrey, J., Pasin, M., Felber, P., Schiavoni, V.: WebAssembly as a common layer for the cloud-edge continuum. In: Proceedings of the 2nd Workshop on Flexible Resource and Application Management on the Edge, pp. 3–8. FRAME, ACM (2022)
22. Ménétrey, J., Pasin, M., Felber, P., et al.: A comprehensive trusted runtime for WebAssembly with Intel SGX. IEEE TDSC **21**, 3562–3579 (2023)
23. OASIS: Topology and Orchestration Specification for Cloud Applications Version 1.0. Oasis standard, OASIS (2013). http://docs.oasis-open.org/tosca/TOSCA/v1.0/os/TOSCA-v1.0-os.html
24. Orive, A., Agirre, A., Truong, H.L.: Quality of service aware orchestration for cloud-edge continuum applications. Sensors **22**(5) (2022)
25. Pahl, C., Lee, B.: Containers and Clusters for Edge Cloud Architectures - A Technology Review (2015)
26. Patros, P., Spillner, J., Papadopoulos, A.V., et al.: Toward sustainable serverless computing. IEEE Internet Comput. **25**, 42–50 (2021)
27. Rocha, I., Göttel, C., Felber, P.: Heats: heterogeneity-and energy-aware task-based scheduling. In: 27th Euromicro International Conference on Parallel, Distributed and Network-Based Processing (PDP), pp. 400–405. IEEE (2019)
28. Sakman, M.C.: CPS orchestrator with distributed image processing pipeline (2026). https://doi.org/10.5281/zenodo.18712919
29. Sakman, M.C., Spillner, J., Schiavoni, V.: Speeding up the development for the computing continuum with WebAssembly. In: 2025 IEEE 30th Pacific Rim International Symposium on Dependable Computing (PRDC), pp. 12–22 (2025)
30. Satyanarayanan, M.: The emergence of edge computing. Computer **50**(1), 30–39 (2017)
31. Shi, W., Cao, J., Zhang, Q., et al.: Edge computing: vision and challenges. IEEE Internet Things J. **3**(5), 637–646 (2016)
32. Tian, K., Ghobaei-Arani, M.: An autonomous energy-aware resource scheduling mechanism in serverless edge computing. Artif. Intell. Rev. **59**, 96 (2026)
33. Vaño, R., Lacalle, I., Sowiński, P.: Cloud-native workload orchestration at the edge: a deployment review and future directions. Sensors **23** (2023)
34. Wang, Z., Goudarzi, M., Aryal, J., Buyya, R.: Container Orchestration in Edge and Fog Computing Environments for Real-Time IoT Applications (2022). https://arxiv.org/abs/2203.05161
35. wasmCloud Project: wasmCloud: A Distributed Application Platform for WebAssembly (2019). https://wasmcloud.com/. Accessed 16 Feb 2026
36. WasmEdge Project: WasmEdge: Lightweight, high-performance WebAssembly runtime (2025). https://wasmedge.org. Accessed 14 Aug 2025
37. Yakubov, D., Hästbacka, D.: Comparative analysis of lightweight kubernetes distributions for edge computing: performance and resource efficiency. In: Pahl, C., Janes, A., Cerny, T., Lenarduzzi, V., Esposito, M. (eds.) Service-Oriented and Cloud Computing. ESOCC 2025. LNCS, vol 15547, pp. 81–95. Springer, Cham (2025). https://doi.org/10.1007/978-3-031-84617-5_7
38. Zhang, Y., Liu, M., Wang, H.: Research on webassembly runtimes: a survey. ACM Trans. Softw. Eng. Methodol. **34** (2025)
39. Čilić, I., Krivić, P., Podnar Žarko, I., Kušek, M.: Performance evaluation of container orchestration tools in edge computing environments. Sensors **23** (2023)

Orbitalis: A Distributed Microkernel Framework

Nicola Ricciardi[iD], Marco Picone[(✉)] [iD], Riccardo Morandi[iD],
and Nicola Bicocchi[iD]

University of Modena and Reggio Emilia, Modena, Italy
`{nicola.ricciardi,marco.picone,riccardo.morandi,`
`nicola.bicocchi}@unimore.it`

Abstract. While the Microkernel paradigm is a cornerstone for achieving modularity and extensibility, its application in modern distributed environments is often hampered by a rigid dependency on specific execution contexts. Existing frameworks often entangle business logic with specific communication technologies, necessitating extensive refactoring when transitioning between monolithic and distributed deployments. In this work, we introduce Orbitalis, an open-source framework that extends the Microkernel paradigm to distributed systems. Orbitalis integrates component development, communication, and lifecycle management, enabling seamless execution across both local and distributed environments, enabling applications to operate seamlessly across heterogeneous nodes without requiring a priori knowledge of the deployment topology. At the heart of the framework lies Busline, an asynchronous, protocol-agnostic publish/subscribe backbone that supports dynamic component evolution, replication, and replacement. A DHCP-inspired discovery protocol enables cores and plugins to negotiate, connect, and reconfigure at runtime. Experimental evaluation quantifies the framework's overhead across various deployment scenarios, demonstrating its practical viability.

1 Introduction

The Microkernel paradigm has long been recognized as an effective solution for achieving modularity and extensibility in software architectures [1]. By isolating a minimal core that provides lifecycle management and essential services from a set of independent plugins, it allows systems to evolve without altering their central logic. This clear separation of concerns reduces coupling, increases maintainability, and enables controlled evolution over time—qualities that are especially valuable in complex, long-lived software systems.

However, traditional microkernel implementations were conceived for single-environment systems, where the core and its plugins coexist within the same execution context and share deterministic communication channels [2]. As modern software increasingly shifts toward decentralized and cloud-native deployments, these localized assumptions are becoming a significant bottleneck. In a

A. Nunes Alonso and R. Palmieri (Eds.): DAIS 2026, LNCS 16591, pp. 89–104, 2026.
https://doi.org/10.1007/978-3-032-27358-1_6

truly distributed landscape, components reside on heterogeneous nodes, communicate asynchronously over unpredictable networks, and must maintain isolation and consistency without the luxury of centralized coordination. At the same time, many contemporary architectures tightly couple their business logic to specific communication protocols or deployment configurations. Adopting technologies such as MQTT [3,4], gRPC [5], or WebSocket [6] often constrains developers to particular interaction patterns and technology stacks. As a result, software systems typically must choose a deployment model a priori—monolithic or distributed—and adapting from one to the other requires significant refactoring and duplication of logic [7]. This rigidity hinders portability and complicates the integration of new functionalities across heterogeneous environments.

The key contribution of this work is Orbitalis, a novel framework that elevates the Microkernel paradigm to a network-transparent abstraction layer. While existing microkernel architectures confine the core/plugin separation to a single process or host, Orbitalis extends this model to distributed environments without requiring developers to anticipate the final deployment topology. Applications developed with Orbitalis run identically whether deployed locally or across a network, removing the boundary between local and distributed system design. This is made possible by three original contributions. First, Busline, a novel asynchronous, multi-channel communication backbone based on the publisher/subscriber pattern, decouples component interaction from any specific transport technology. Unlike existing message-passing or RPC-based solutions, Busline allows components to exchange events transparently across heterogeneous protocols and infrastructures, enabling deployment-agnostic communication by design. Second, Orbitalis introduces a distributed-ready microkernel architecture that preserves the classical separation between core and plugins while extending it with flexible component granularity and independent lifecycle control: each component can evolve, replicate, or be replaced dynamically without compromising system stability—a property that centralized or statically configured frameworks do not provide. Third, the framework introduces runtime discovery and negotiation mechanisms that allow cores and plugins to identify and connect at runtime, enabling genuine hot-plugging, self-healing behaviors, and continuous reconfiguration. This supports the development of long-lived, self-adapting distributed systems that existing plugin-based frameworks are not designed to address.

The remainder of this paper is structured as follows. Section 2 surveys related technologies and frameworks, highlighting how *Orbitalis* differentiates itself from existing approaches. Section 3 introduces *Busline*, the event-driven communication backbone enabling asynchronous interactions. Section 4 describes the overall *Orbitalis* architecture, detailing the relationships and responsibilities of cores and plugins in both local and distributed deployments and presents the dynamic discovery and runtime plugging protocol, which supports autonomous configuration and self-healing behavior. Section 5 explains the interaction semantics between cores and plugins, illustrating how operations are executed and synchronized through event exchange while Sect. 6 details their interactions during

Table 1. Comparison between Orbitalis and related frameworks.

Framework	Primary Goal	Distributed	Discovery & Negotiation	Comm. Model	Limitations
Pluggy (Python)	Plugin extensibility via hook registry	No	No	Synchronous, in-process calls	Local-only, no runtime negotiation or event abstraction
Apache Camel	Message routing and protocol integration	Partial	Pre-configured endpoints only	Message routing with connectors	No autonomous discovery; topology defined upfront
Volttron	Distributed multi-agent platform for automation	Yes (broker-based)	Centralized VIP registry	Pub/Sub via RabbitMQ or ZeroMQ	Requires broker, lacks peer-to-peer discovery
ZeroMQ/ZRE	Low-level messaging transport and patterns	Yes	Limited (focus on transport)	Asynchronous sockets	No lifecycle, schema or plugin negotiation layer
OSGi/Apache Celix	Dynamic modularity in a shared runtime	Local JVM/process	Central service registry	In-process service calls	No distributed plugin model; single-runtime assumption
Akka/Orleans	Actor-based distributed systems	Yes	Registry-driven runtime discovery	Async message passing	Persistent actors, not ephemeral plugins; discovery not protocol-level
Orbitalis	Unified microkernel spanning local and distributed deployments	Yes (fully peer-to-peer)	Autonomous, protocol-level negotiation	Event-driven, transport agnostic (Busline)	*– extends microkernel principles beyond single-host execution* *–*

application evolution and execution. Section 7 reports the experimental evaluation of *Orbitalis*, analyzing its performance, overhead, and scalability under different deployment scenarios. Finally, Sect. 8 concludes the paper, summarizing the main contributions and outlining future directions for extending the *Orbitalis* framework toward fully adaptive distributed systems.

2 Related Work

Several frameworks and middleware platforms have been developed to support modularity, dynamic extensibility, and distributed communication in software architectures. While *Orbitalis* shares conceptual similarities with these systems, it distinguishes itself by unifying microkernel-style modularity across both local and distributed deployments. In contrast to solutions that depend on centralized registries, static configuration, or host-bound execution, *Orbitalis* introduces native, protocol-level discoverability that elevates discovery and negotiation to first-class mechanisms, enabling dynamic composition and runtime hot-plugging of components. Its event-driven, transport-agnostic communication layer decouples system behavior from the underlying networking technologies, allowing seamless adaptation, flexibility across heterogeneous environments, and the reuse of components across diverse deployment scenarios (Table 1).

Pluggy is a lightweight plugin management system for Python applications such as pytest [8,9]. It enables modular extension through a registry of hooks, allowing dynamic function calls within a single runtime process. Each plugin registers functions corresponding to these hooks, which the host program can invoke at runtime. Unlike *Orbitalis*, Pluggy is entirely local and synchronous, lacking distributed discovery, runtime hot-plugging, or event-driven communication. It focuses on code-level extensibility rather than runtime interoperability across networked nodes.

Apache Camel provides integration via message routing, protocol adaptation, and data transformation [10,11]. Its routes define message flows between components, using connectors for protocols such as HTTP, MQTT, Kafka, or JMS. While Camel assumes preconfigured endpoints and static routing, *Orbitalis* introduces autonomous discovery and negotiation among dynamically instantiated components, allowing them to connect and reconfigure at runtime without centralized orchestration.

VOLTTRON is a distributed multi-agent platform for energy management and building automation [12,13]. Agents communicate through a message bus and register capabilities via topics using a centralized protocol (VIP). Discovery is coordinated via a central broker, and communication relies on RabbitMQ or ZeroMQ. In contrast, *Orbitalis* employs a decentralized, DHCP-like discovery protocol, enabling peer-to-peer negotiation and dynamic reconfiguration of plugins without requiring a centralized message broker.

ZeroMQ is a low-level, brokerless messaging library supporting publish/subscribe and request/reply patterns [14,15]. While *Orbitalis* could use ZeroMQ as a transport layer, it operates at a higher level of abstraction, handling component lifecycle management, runtime schema validation, negotiation, and hot-plugging of distributed modules, in addition to message delivery.

OSGi and Apache Celix define dynamic component models for the Java ecosystem, enabling runtime installation, activation, and removal of modular bundles [16,17]. OSGi bundles register services in a centralized registry and communicate via in-process calls. In contrast, *Orbitalis* extends modularity across distributed nodes with event-driven communication, enabling independent cores to discover and interact with plugins dynamically, supporting replication, replacement, and protocol-agnostic communication.

Akka and Microsoft Orleans implement the Actor Model for high-concurrency, stateful distributed entities [18,19]. Actors (or Grains) maintain persistent state and communicate asynchronously through message passing. Like these frameworks, *Orbitalis* is event-driven and decentralized, but its plugins are ephemeral operational providers rather than persistent actors. Its discovery and negotiation protocol is lightweight and ephemeral, emphasizing runtime adaptability and autonomous reconfiguration over long-lived state management or cluster membership maintenance.

3   Communication Backbone: Busline

At the core of *Orbitalis* is *Busline*, a flexible, protocol-agnostic communication layer implementing a distributed asynchronous publish/subscribe model. Busline provides a unified interface independent of transport technologies, enabling modular, event-driven architectures that are network-transparent. It abstracts message routing and delivery, allowing Cores and Plugins to interact seamlessly across local and distributed deployments.

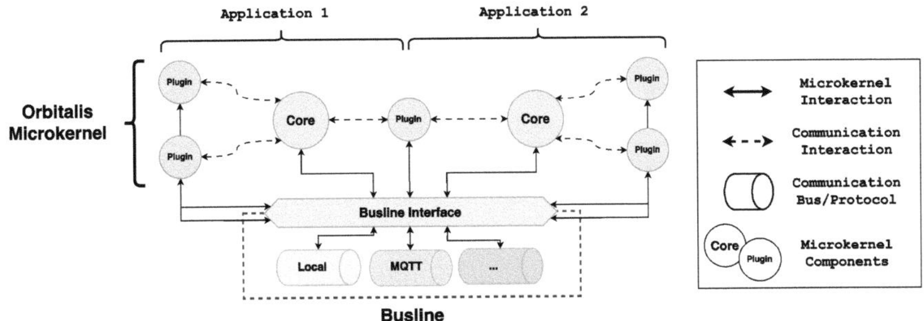

Fig. 1. Conceptual overview of the relationship between Orbitalis and Busline.

3.1   Asynchronous Publish/Subscribe Paradigm

Communication in *Orbitalis* is fully asynchronous. Messages are published as events to specific topics, which subscribers—local or remote—handle independently. This design allows concurrent operations, improves throughput, and increases resilience to network latency. By decoupling publishers from subscribers, new components can join or leave dynamically without disrupting existing flows, promoting loose coupling and system evolution.

3.2   Message Handling and Event Semantics

Each Busline event consists of a Message, containing the payload, and an Event, containing metadata such as publisher identifiers and timestamps. This separation improves traceability and supports monitoring and auditing. Busline employs Avro-based serialization, enforcing schema validation at both ends of communication to prevent mismatches and ensure interoperability. This also enables backward-compatible incremental schema evolution, essential for long-lived distributed systems.

3.3   Unified Event Bus Abstraction

Busline provides a unified abstraction over multiple transport technologies, including in-memory event buses and distributed brokers such as MQTT (Fig. 1). Events can propagate through multiple channels simultaneously—for example, locally for low-latency communication while also reaching remote subscribers. Busline manages these multi-channel interactions transparently, ensuring consistency and isolation across communication domains. This capability allows *Orbitalis* to operate efficiently across heterogeneous networks, combining low-latency local communication with globally scalable, fault-tolerant distributed messaging.

4   Orbitalis Architecture

The *Orbitalis* framework is based on a microkernel architecture that decouples core system logic from domain-specific functionalities. Its design revolves around two primary entities: Cores and Plugins. Together, they form a dynamic ecosystem with clearly partitioned responsibilities, event-driven communication, and inherent runtime adaptability.

4.1   Core–Plugin Model

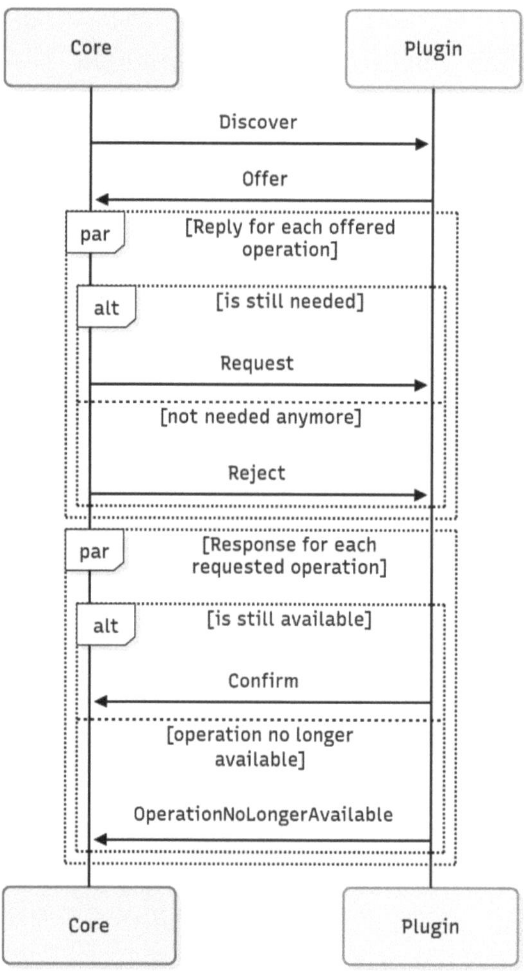

Fig. 2. Sequence diagram illustrating the handshaking protocol between the Core and the Plugin.

In this model, the Core provides minimal mechanisms to maintain system stability and interface with external modules, while Plugins extend the Core with domain-specific functionality. Each Plugin exposes operations that Cores can invoke remotely, effectively acting as service providers in a distributed environment. This separation allows Cores to orchestrate functionality while Plugins provide capabilities. Communication is entirely asynchronous and message-oriented, avoiding the tight coupling typical of RPC or API-based approaches. This design ensures high modularity and independence among system components.

4.2 Multi-core and Multi-domain Topology

Orbitalis supports multiple Cores and Plugins operating concurrently across different network domains. Each Core can connect to multiple Plugins, and each Plugin can serve multiple Cores, forming a distributed mesh with dynamic coordination. Scalability is enhanced by the Busline event system, which allows messages to be exchanged over multiple channels, such as local in-process buses or MQTT brokers. This ensures seamless interaction across heterogeneous networks, while decoupling message transport from business logic. Hybrid deployments are supported, enabling low-latency local operations alongside scalable remote coordination. All communication occurs via events—serialized messages following standardized schemas, typically Avro. Each event encapsulates payload and metadata, such as sender identifiers and timestamps, ensuring interoperability, schema validation, and traceable message flows. The reactive, actor-inspired model fosters concurrency, loose coupling, and resilience.

5   Dynamic Discovery and Runtime Plugging

A key feature of *Orbitalis* is its ability to dynamically discover, connect, and configure components at runtime without requiring system restarts. This is achieved through a discovery protocol inspired by DHCP, which allows Cores and Plugins to identify one another, negotiate compatibility, and establish connections autonomously. This mechanism forms the foundation of Orbitalis's hot-plugging capability, enabling components to join or leave while the system remains active. Unlike traditional architectures with static bindings, Orbitalis treats system topology as dynamic and self-organizing. Cores broadcast discovery messages to announce their presence and request available operations, while Plugins respond with offers describing their capabilities. This continuous exchange maintains an updated map of operations and resources across distributed nodes, minimizing downtime and reducing manual intervention.

The discovery process follows a four-phase handshake (illustrated in Fig. 2):

1. *Discover* – Core broadcasts a request with required operations and metadata.
2. *Offer* – Plugins reply with available operations and constraints.
3. *Reply* – Core accepts or rejects offered operations via Request or Reject messages.

4. *Response* – Plugins finalize negotiation with Confirm or OperationNoLonger-Available messages.

Discovery is continuous, providing self-healing capabilities. If a Plugin fails or disconnects, Cores detect the absence via keepalive signals and initiate new discovery sessions. Newly introduced Plugins can announce themselves, prompting Cores to establish connections automatically. The protocol uses compact Avro-serialized messages. This allows multiple concurrent negotiations, supporting scalability as the number of components grows. Its schema-based design ensures extensibility for future features.

6   Cores-Plugins Interaction

In *Orbitalis*, both cores and plugins can be considered as state machines with distinct transitions. This section describes these state machines and the runtime interaction pattern used to execute operations and collect results. The presentation is conceptual and transport-agnostic; references to message formats and topics are at the protocol level (e.g., schema-typed messages, input/output topics) rather than implementation-specific details.

Cores and Plugins expose lifecycle hooks and message-level hooks (e.g., on start, on request, on reply, on close) that allow instrumentation, logging, metrics collection, and custom policy enforcement. Hooks are invoked at well-defined points in state transitions and operation flow and provide the recommended extension points for monitoring, tracing, or custom reconciliation logic.

6.1   Core States and Transitions

Cores are configured with operation requirements specifying the operations a core must satisfy, including minimum/maximum plugin counts, mandatory or allowed plugin identifiers, and accepted input/output schemas. This allows a core to manage multiple plugins that expose the same operation name but with different inputs and outputs, similar to overloading and polymorphism in OOP. When requirements are satisfied, a core becomes *compliant*, and this transition (as well as others) can be intercepted to trigger specific business logic.

- *CREATED:* Core instantiated, identifiers and configuration set, and event-bus clients initialized. Discovery and operation acceptance may not yet have started.
- *COMPLIANT/NOT-COMPLIANT:* After discovery and negotiation, the core evaluates compliance for each required operation set. If all requirements are met, it is compliant; if not, it is not-compliant. Compliance is dynamic and context-dependent: a core may be compliant for some operations and not for others.
- *STOPPED:* Core terminates its event loop, closes connections, unsubscribes from discovery topics, and releases resources. Transition may result from a controlled shutdown or forced termination.

6.2 Plugin States and Transitions

Plugins also have configuration and policies that define how connection requests are handled, including allowlists, blocklists, or maximum numbers of connections per operation.

- *CREATED:* Plugin instantiated, operations and policies populated. Ready to advertise capabilities but not yet running.
- *RUNNING:* Plugin active, subscribes to inbound topics, listens to discovery messages, responds with offers, accepts requests, processes events, and produces outputs. Event loop is active.
- *STOPPED:* Plugin stops operation, unsubscribes from topics, closes connections, and releases resources.

Plugins may advertise changes in their offered operations while running (e.g., temporarily disabling an operation). These changes are signaled via Offer or OperationNoLongerAvailable messages, prompting cores to re-evaluate connected operations.

6.3 Operation Execution

This subsection details the protocol for executing an operation provided by a plugin and collecting results at the core. Discovery and connection establishment are assumed complete. Each connection represents a channel between a core and a plugin for a specific operation name and schema. Multiple connections between the same core and plugin are allowed if they represent different operations or schema variants. Connections include metadata such as input/output topics, expected schemas, timestamps, and flags indicating whether output is expected.

Request Preparation (Core Side). The core determines the operation to execute and selects all active connections matching the operation name and intended input topic. Based on the selected mode (*all, any,* specific plugin ID, or an algorithm such as round-robin or least-recently-used), a subset of connections is used. The core then prepares and sends the operation input via Busline's infrastructure. If the operation has no input, a payload-less event is sent. Asynchronous messaging allows the core to continue other tasks without blocking.

Connection Locking and Touching. For each selected connection, the core acquires a connection lock to prevent concurrent conflicts and updates the *last use* attribute, keeping the connection active and avoiding premature closure.

Operation Execution. Plugins subscribed to the input topic receive the event and dispatch it to the corresponding handler, executing the operation logic. Periodic operations with no input may trigger handlers internally. If outputs are expected, the plugin publishes results to the associated output topic.

Core Collection. The core collects output events via Busline subscriptions, correlates responses with the original request using identifiers (request ID, operation name, connection ID), and processes results. Afterwards, connection locks are released and the *last use* property is updated.

7 Experimental Evaluation

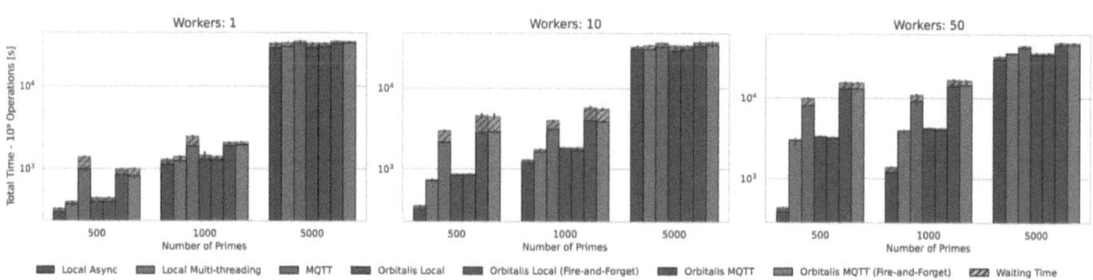

Fig. 3. Total and CPU execution time (in seconds) in local and MQTT scenarios, considering one million operations.

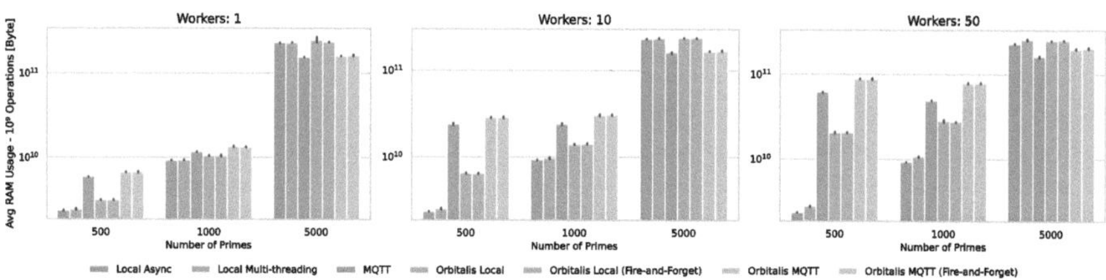

Fig. 4. Average RAM utilization (in bytes) in local and MQTT scenarios, considering one million operations.

This section presents the performance evaluation of the proposed system, comparing the Orbitalis framework with traditional approaches that do not rely on this library. The experimental scenario involves two primary classes: *Worker* and *Coordinator*. The objective of the simulation is the computation of prime numbers. The *Coordinator* is responsible for partitioning the overall workload into smaller tasks and distributing them to multiple *Workers*. Each *Worker* computes the prime numbers within its assigned numerical interval, and upon completion, the *Coordinator* collects and stores the results.

The *Coordinator* and *Worker* classes were implemented using different architectural approaches. The first implementation is based on the Orbitalis library, where the *Coordinator* class extends the *Core* class and the *Worker* class extends the *Plugin* class provided by Orbitalis. Additionally, three alternative implementations not based on Orbitalis were developed to enable a comprehensive comparison.

These include a local asynchronous approach, a local multithreaded approach, and a distributed solution based on MQTT communication. Furthermore two communication buses have been evaluated: a local bus, for comparison with the local execution scenarios, and an MQTT-based bus, for comparison with the distributed MQTT solution.

7.1 Execution Performance Analysis

We conducted a comprehensive set of experiments to evaluate the performance of Orbitalis in comparison with non-Orbitalis approaches, including the worst cases for Orbitalis, where really low computation is needed. All the scenarios described in the following were implemented under different configurations, namely: *Orbitalis Local, Orbitalis Local with fire-and-forget mode, Local Async, Local Multithread, Orbitalis MQTT, Oribtalis MQTT with fire-and-forget mode* and *MQTT*. These experiments were designed to assess the behavior of the framework under multiple execution and communication conditions.

Each scenario was tested using a variable number of *Worker* instances, specifically 1, 10, and 50 workers. In addition, the prime number computation task was performed by computing all prime numbers up to 500, 1000, and 5000. For each experimental configuration, the reported values represent the average of one million iterations. Each experiment was repeated 5 times to also evaluate the variability of the collected data.

The first performance analysis focuses on the total execution time of the experiments. In this case, execution time is defined as the total duration, expressed in seconds, required to complete one million iterations of the prime number computation, where each iteration computes up to N prime numbers. For this analysis, both the total wall-clock time and the total CPU time were measured.

Figure 3 reports the results obtained for the different configurations in the local and MQTT execution scenarios. From left to right, the figure shows the behaviour of the different implementations as the number of *Worker* instances used to split the computational load increases.

In the case of a single worker in local scenarios, the Orbitalis-based implementations exhibit performance that is comparable to the non-Orbitalis solutions, even as the number of prime numbers to be computed increases. When considering 10 and 50 workers, the *Local Async* solution achieves better performance for smaller input sizes, that is, when a lower number of prime numbers is computed. This behaviour is due to the fact that the *Local Async* implementation does not require data exchange over a local communication bus needed for decoupling, resulting in lower overhead and higher efficiency in lightweight workloads. However, as the computational load increases, the performance of Orbitalis becomes fully aligned with that of the non-Orbitalis implementations.

Even in MQTT scenarios, from left to right, the Fig. 3 reports different scenarios obtained by increasing the number of *Worker* instances. In the single-worker configuration, the Orbitalis-based implementation shows execution times that are comparable with those of the non-Orbitalis solution. As the number of workers increases, a behaviour similar to the local scenario can be observed. For smaller computational loads, that is, when a lower number of prime numbers is computed, the Orbitalis-based version exhibits higher CPU execution times. However, as the number of prime numbers to be computed increases, this performance gap becomes less significant.

An additional performance analysis concerns memory usage across the different scenarios. All previously described configurations were tested in local and MQTT execution scenarios. The results obtained are reported in Fig. 4. From left to right, the figure shows the behavior of the different implementations as the number of *Worker* instances increases, similarly to the previous analyses.

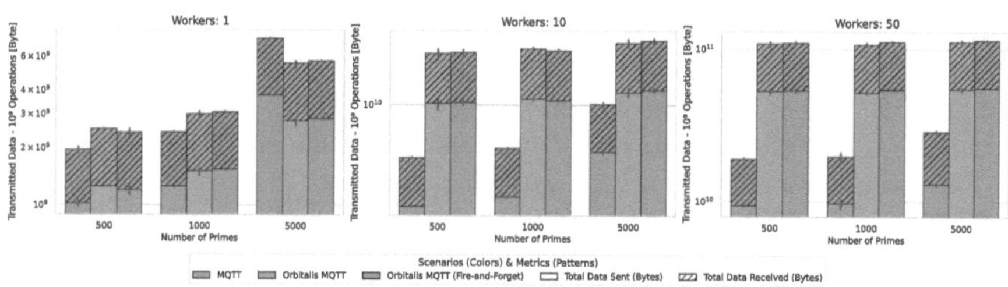

Fig. 5. Transferred and received data (in bytes) in MQTT scenarios, considering one million operations.

In local scenarios, with a single worker, even as the number of prime numbers to be computed increases, the memory usage in bytes remains comparable between the non-Orbitalis local solutions and the Orbitalis-based local implementation using the communication bus. As the number of workers increases, the Orbitalis framework must store in memory the information required by the *Core* to maintain the connections with the *Plugins*, resulting in a bit more memory consumption.

However, as the computational load increases, that is, as the number of prime numbers grows, the memory usage of the Orbitalis-based solution becomes progressively more aligned with that of the non-Orbitalis implementations. This behaviour indicates that the memory overhead introduced by the framework becomes negligible for larger workloads.

In the single-worker MQTT configuration, the Orbitalis-based implementations exhibits a memory usage that is comparable to that of the non-Orbitalis version. As the number of workers increases, a higher memory consumption can be observed for the Orbitalis-based solution, particularly in the case where 500 prime numbers are computed. Even in this case, higher memory consumption is likely due to connections information storing needs, which allows Orbitalis to manage *Plugins*.

For the MQTT-based scenario, an additional analysis was performed on the number of transmitted and received packets, since this configuration involves a distributed computation. Figure 5 shows the comparison between *Orbitalis*

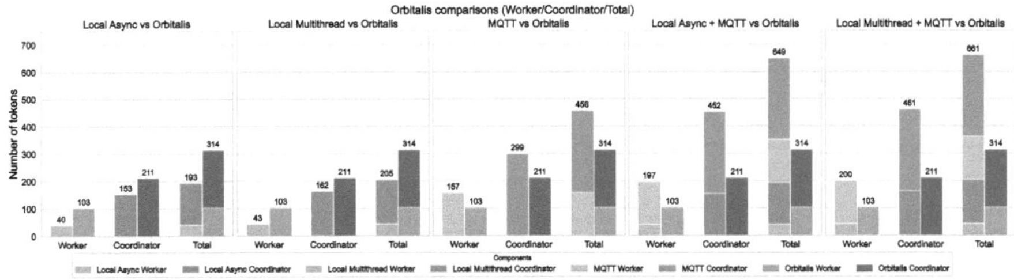

Fig. 6. Python token count comparison for the *Worker* and *Coordinator* classes across different implementation approaches.

MQTT and the non-Orbitalis MQTT implementation in terms of data transmission and reception. As in the previous analyses, from left to right the figure shows the behavior of the different implementations as the number of *Worker* instances increases.

We must consider that in non-Orbitalis implementation a very simple communication protocol is simulated, where start and end of prime numbers computation range are sent separated by a comma (e.g. "*1,9*" which requires only three bytes). Instead, Orbitalis relies on Avro to serialize structured messages before sending them and when this leads in measurable overhead when message payloads are very tiny.

In the single-worker configuration, the amount of transmitted and received data remains comparable between the Orbitalis-based and the non-Orbitalis implementations given the limited number of exchanged messages. Instead, when the number of workers increases, a growing gap can be observed, given that more small messages are sent.

We have also evaluated Orbitalis in scenarios in which messages are more complex and require more data. In this cases Avro serialization helps to reduce total amount of exchanged data, becoming more convenient than raw messages.

Finally, a further performance analysis focuses on the discovery phase of the framework. This analysis evaluates the time required by Orbitalis to complete the discovery of the *Worker* instances (i.e., plugins) under different numbers of workers. We also evaluated the time required to complete the discovery phase as a function of the number of *Worker* instances used in the previously described configurations, considering both the local and the MQTT-based versions.

In the local scenario, the discovery time is in the order of milliseconds. Specifically, it is approximately 1 ms for a single worker, 4 ms for 10 workers, and 13 ms for 50 workers. In the MQTT-based scenario, the discovery time is also in the order of milliseconds, with values of approximately 54 ms for a single worker, 19 ms for 10 workers, and 75 ms for 50 workers. This analysis shows that the discovery phase introduces a measurable delay, which however remains very limited. For the majority of practical applications, this overhead can be considered negligible with respect to the overall execution time of the system.

7.2   Source Code Token Analysis

The final analysis focuses on the Python token count of the *Worker* and *Coordinator* classes, as well as on their total combined size. Figure 6 reports several comparisons between the Orbitalis-based implementation and the non-Orbitalis solutions.

The first plot on the left compares the number of tokens required by the *Worker* and *Coordinator* classes in the local asynchronous version and in the Orbitalis-based version. In this case, the Orbitalis implementation presents a higher code complexity. This is mainly due to the additional method calls required by the framework to manage communication over the local bus, while the non-framework implementation does not need to handle this level of abstraction. A similar behavior can be observed in the second plot, where the local multithreaded version is compared against the Orbitalis-based implementation. Also in this case, the Orbitalis solution requires more tokens due to the framework-related communication mechanisms.

In contrast, the third plot shows that Orbitalis requires fewer tokens than the MQTT-based implementation without the framework. This result highlights that, in a distributed scenario, Orbitalis helps the developer by abstracting and hiding part of the communication complexity, thus reducing the overall code size. Finally, the last two plots compare scenarios in which both a local and an MQTT-based version are required within the same experimental setup. In this case, the non-Orbitalis solution shows a significantly higher complexity, since the developer must implement two separate versions of the *Worker* and *Coordinator* classes. By contrast, when using Orbitalis, a single implementation is sufficient to handle both communication modes.

8   Conclusion

In this paper, we presented *Orbitalis*, an open-source software framework that extends the Microkernel paradigm to distributed systems. By unifying component development, communication, and lifecycle management, it enables seamless execution across both local and distributed environments, allowing developers to focus on functionality rather than deployment intricacies.

The proposed approach demonstrates that the core principles of the Microkernel paradigm can be effectively generalized to distributed software ecosystems. Through the *Busline* communication layer, *Orbitalis* abstracts over multiple transport technologies, providing a unified, asynchronous backbone for message exchange that decouples system behavior from network implementation details. The framework's DHCP-like discovery mechanism supports autonomous negotiation and runtime composition of components, enabling systems to evolve and adapt dynamically without requiring downtime. Together, these features foster a self-organizing, fault-tolerant architecture in which cores and plugins can dynamically adjust to operational contexts, resource availability, and network conditions. By decoupling functionality from deployment topology, *Orbitalis* allows software to shift fluidly between monolithic and distributed configurations through simple reconfiguration rather than redesign. This capability offers a substantial advantage for applications spanning domains such as IoT orchestration, cloud-native services, robotics, and cyber-physical infrastructures. Additionally, the framework encourages code reuse and extensibility, simplifying the integration of new components and enabling heterogeneous environments to interoperate seamlessly.

Future work will focus on broadening the applicability of *Orbitalis* by providing extended support for multiple programming languages for both cores and plugins, alongside a systematic experimental evaluation to assess performance, interoperability, and development complexity. Moreover, we plan to validate the framework in realistic Cyber-Physical Systems (CPS) [20] and Digital Twins [21] use cases and deployments, exploring its effectiveness in dynamic, large-scale, and safety-critical scenarios.

References

1. Liedtke, J.: On microkernel construction. In: Proceedings of the 15th ACM Symposium on Operating Systems Principles (SOSP) (1995)
2. Maier, W., Pohlmann, N., Reiser, H.: Microkernel-based distributed systems: an overview. J. Syst. Architect. **96**, 1–14 (2019)
3. Banks, A., Gupta, R.: MQTT version 5.0 (2019). https://docs.oasis-open.org/mqtt/mqtt/v5.0/mqtt-v5.0.html. OASIS Standard, Tech. Rep
4. Hunkeler, U., Truong, H.L., Stanford-Clark, A.: MQTT-s – a publish/subscribe protocol for wireless sensor networks. In: Proceedings of the 3rd International Conference on Communication Systems Software and Middleware (2008)
5. gRPC Authors, "grpc core protocol specification (2023). https://github.com/grpc/grpc/blob/master/doc/PROTOCOL-HTTP2.md. Accessed 01 Nov 2025
6. Fette, I., Melnikov, A.: The WebSocket protocol. RFC 6455, (2011) Internet Engineering Task Force (IETF
7. Dragoni, N., Lanese, I., Larsen, S., Mazzara, M., Mustafin, R., Safina, L.: Microservices: yesterday, today, and tomorrow. In: Present and Ulterior Software Engineering, Springer (2017)
8. Krekel, H., et al.: Pluggy: a minimalist production ready plugin system (2017). https://pluggy.readthedocs.io/en/stable/. Accessed 01 Nov 2025
9. —, "pytest: simple powerful testing with python," https://docs.pytest.org/en/latest/. pluggy is the underlying plugin system used by pytest
10. Ibsen, C., Anstey, J.: Camel in Action. Manning Publications (2010)
11. Apache Software Foundation, "Apache camel documentation" (2025). https://camel.apache.org/. Accessed 01 Nov 2025
12. Haack, J.N., Kalsi, K., Pratt, R., Hammerstrom, D.: VOLTTRON: an agent platform for integrating electric vehicles and smart grid. In: Proceedings of the IEEE PES Innovative Smart Grid Technologies Conference (ISGT), (2013)
13. Pacific Northwest National Laboratory, "VOLTTRON documentation" (2025). https://volttron.readthedocs.io/. Accessed 01 Nov 2025
14. Hintjens, P.: ZeroMQ: Messaging for Many Applications. O'Reilly Media (2013)
15. ZeroMQ Project, "ZeroMQ documentation" (2025). https://zeromq.org/. Accessed 01 Nov 2025

16. Hall, R.S., Pauls, K., McCulloch, S., Savage, D.: OSGi in Action: Creating Modular Applications in Java. Manning Publications (2011)
17. Apache Software Foundation, "Apache Celix documentation" (2025). https://celix.apache.org/. Accessed 01 Nov 2025
18. Roestenburg, R., Bakker, R., Williams, R.: Akka in Action. Manning Publications (2016)
19. Bernstein, P., Bykov, S., Geller, A., Kliot, G., Thelin, J.: Orleans: distributed virtual actors for programmability and scalability. In: Proceedings of the 2nd ACM Symposium on Cloud Computing (SoCC '11, (2011)
20. Moreno Molina, J., Ferrer García, J., Kuchkovsky Jiménez, C.: Archer: an event-driven architecture for cyber-physical systems. In: IEEE/ACM International Conference on Utility and Cloud Computing Companion (UCC Companion), pp. 335–340. (2018)
21. Martinelli, M., Barbone, A., Morandi, R., Picone, M., Burattini, S., Ricci, A.: Modular engineering of industrial digital twins: the WLDT approach. In: 2025 21st International Conference on Distributed Computing in Smart Systems and the Internet of Things (DCOSS-IoT), pp. 451–458. (2025)

An Automated IoT-Based Infrastructure for Real-Time Soil Water Deficit Prediction
(Use-Case Paper)

Michèle Fischer[1], Hugo Delottier[1], Qi Tang[2], Oliver S. Schilling[2],
Valerio Schiavoni[1(✉)], and Philip Brunner[1]

[1] University of Neuchâtel, Neuchâtel, Switzerland
`{michele.fischer,hugo.delottier,valerio.schiavoni,`
`philip.brunner}@unine.ch`
[2] University of Basel, Basel, Switzerland
`{Qi.Tang,oliver.schilling}@unibas.ch`

Abstract. In Switzerland, 80% of drinking water originates from groundwater. In the current context of climate change, the pressure on water resources and agricultural demand is increasing which highlights the need for better irrigation management. Quantifying soil water deficit with almost real-time constraints leads to improved irrigation decisions while limiting unnecessary water use.

This case-study paper presents the design, implementation and evaluation of an automated system for estimating soil water deficit using environmental sensor data, meteorological data, and hydrological modelling. The system integrates in-situ soil moisture measurements with meteorological data from MeteoSwiss. These measurements and data are stored in a time-series database and processed to generate input files for physics based models jointly simulating surface water and groundwater. We describe in detail the operation workflow of our system in this specific use-case, including model simulations, and the required data transfers. The results show that the system operates reliably and provides consistent outputs suitable for short-term soil water deficit estimation.

Keywords: IoT-based infrastructure · environmental and meteorological time-series · physics-based models · agricultural water management

1 Introduction

In Switzerland, around 80% of drinking water originates from groundwater [26]. At the same time, climate change–induced droughts are increasing irrigation demand, which is largely met by groundwater resources. As a result, groundwater plays a dual role as a primary source for both drinking water supply and agricultural irrigation. Combined with population growth, this rising dependence intensifies pressure on groundwater resources and increases the potential for use conflicts.

© IFIP International Federation for Information Processing 2026
Published by Springer Nature Switzerland AG 2026
A. Nunes Alonso and R. Palmieri (Eds.): DAIS 2026, LNCS 16591, pp. 105–120, 2026.
https://doi.org/10.1007/978-3-032-27358-1_7

In this context, the Swiss government adopted a concrete Action Plan [7] for 2020–2025. A key objective is to reduce irrigation without reducing the crop yield. Predicting soil water dynamics and therefore, irrigation needs is essential in this regard. The amount of soil water available to plants results from a complex interplay between precipitation, evaporative losses, and plant uptake dynamics and is strongly controlled by soil properties such as texture, structure, and hydraulic conductivity, which govern water storage and transport. In shallow groundwater systems, soil moisture is further influenced by capillary rise from the water table, whereby upward water movement replenishes moisture in the root zone. This process can increase the water available to crops and reduce irrigation requirements during dry periods [18,34].

Soil moisture sensors enable real-time assessment of water conditions in the root zone and provide valuable information on plant water availability. Using these observations together with predefined soil hydraulic properties, metrics such as soil water deficit (SWD) can be computed to evaluate current irrigation needs [21]. However, while sensors provide information on current conditions, anticipating soil moisture dynamics over the coming days requires accounting for upcoming weather conditions, particularly precipitation and evaporation. This forecasting enables the delivery of an optimized amount of irrigation to maintain soil moisture levels that are optimal for crop growth.

To support such predictions, soil models are increasingly used in agricultural water management (e.g., smart agriculture 4.0 [30]), often driven by short-term weather forecasts to anticipate crop water stress before critical thresholds are reached. Soil models are based on differential equations describing water movement through variably saturated soils [33]. However, most models currently employed in precision agriculture neglect groundwater, despite its important role in sustaining soil moisture through capillary rise. Explicitly accounting for groundwater in existing modelling frameworks enables a more holistic representation of soil moisture dynamics by capturing interactions between the unsaturated zone and the water table. However, although such models exist [29], they currently lack real-time operational architectures that allow continuous data integration and forecasting.

Implementing such a simulation framework requires a robust Internet of Things (IoT) infrastructure to ensure near real-time data streaming from remote sensors and weather forecast products.

In this use-case paper, we describe the design, implementation and evaluation of an IoT-based infrastructure to support the quantification of irrigation demand (i.e., SWD) in near real-time (i.e., daily updates) using a mechanistic soil model simulating soil moisture dynamics under consideration of capillary rise through groundwater, plant water uptake and forecasted weather data. Our architecture supports the prediction of SWD (further described in Sect. 2.2) for five days, using a daily time-step. More specifically, we base our simulation framework on meteorological data and weather forecasts (from a public web-service, i.e., the Federal Office of Meteorology and Climatology MeteoSwiss [6]) and real-time environmental data from remote sensors provided by Decentlab [8]. Meteorological data include precipitation and potential *evapotranspiration* (as explained later in Sect. 2.1). The sensors installed in the field provide real-time data on soil moisture and the level of groundwater, obtained through measuring water pressure (see Sect. 2.2). We store these data series in a highly optimized time-series database, e.g., InfluxDB [16].

We describe our software architecture, the interaction with external web-services, and the integration with mechanistic soil models. The main contribution of this use-case paper is the coupling of an IoT-based infrastructure to a mechanistic soil model accounting for shallow groundwater conditions in an operational agricultural water management implementation.

Roadmap. The remainder of this paper is organized as follows. Section 2 introduces the required agro-meterological terminology and processes. Section 3 describes the design of the proposed software architecture, providing information on the nature of IoT data acquired by the remote sensors, the data sources from MeteoSwiss, and the operations from the physical models. We give implementation details in Sect. 4. Section 5 presents the results obtained from the real-world deployment of the system. We conclude and describe future work in Sect. 6.

2 Agro-Meterological Terminology and Processes

In this section, we briefly describe the meteorological and environmental data required to establish a precision agriculture system. The relevant processes are illustrated in Fig. 1. All processes shown in Fig. 1 are explicitly simulated in the HydroGeoSphere [2] modelling framework employed in this study.

2.1 Weather Forcing

Weather forcing is required to impose dynamic changes to our modelling framework. In soil models, weather dynamics are the primary variable driving the soil moisture conditions. That is, because weather conditions can change very dynamically, the forcing is updated on a daily basis to cope with complex dynamic changes of weather conditions.

Precipitation (P) refers to the water released from the atmosphere in the form of rainfall or snowfall that reaches the Earth's surface. It represents a key input to the hydrological cycle and strongly influences soil moisture and groundwater recharge. Precipitation is typically measured at weather stations using rain gauges and is also estimated in weather forecasts.

Evapotranspiration (ET) is the combined loss of water through soil evaporation and plant transpiration [1]. Potential evapotranspiration (PET) represents the maximum water loss under given weather conditions, assuming unlimited water supply, and is typically estimated from meteorological variables [19]. Actual evapotranspiration (AET) reflects real conditions and is lower than PET when water is limited, for example, due to soil moisture deficits. Numerical models such as HydroGeoSphere calculate AET based on PET and soil water conditions. As precipitation, PET is provided in weather forecasts.

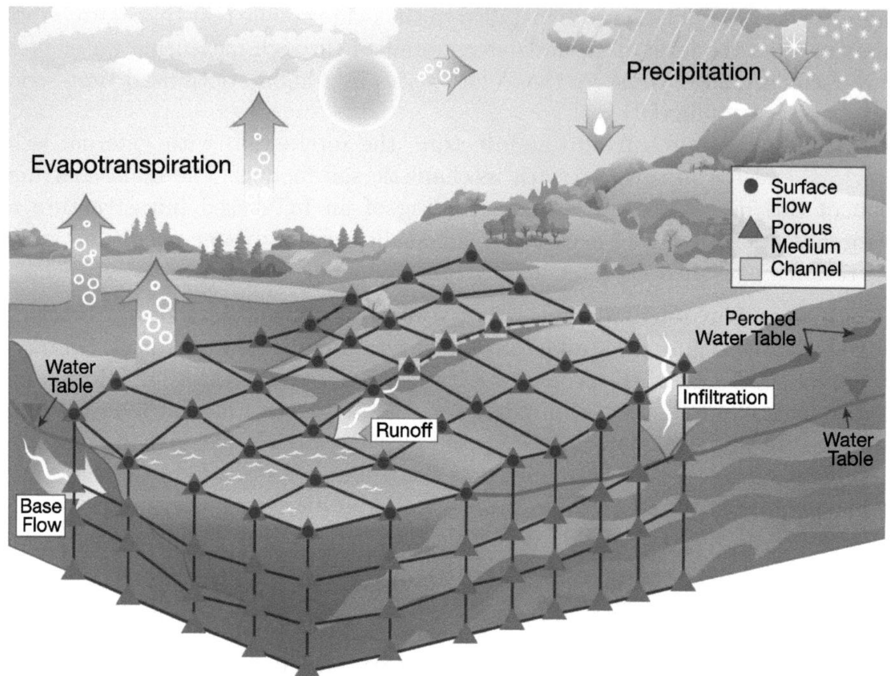

Fig. 1. Hydrological processes implemented in the HydroGeoSphere environment [3].

2.2   Soil Physics Terminology and State Variables

Pores are the spaces available between soil particles. Porosity is a measure of the void spaces or pores within a soil, expressed as a fraction or percentage of the total volume.

Volumetric Water Content (VWC) is the total volumetric amount of water stored in a given volume of soil. A related quantity is the degree of saturation, which varies between 0 to 1. At full saturation, the entire pore volume is filled with water.

Field Capacity (FC) is a defined soil moisture threshold above which excess water in the soil is drained by gravity. It is a concept mainly used in agriculture to support the estimation of soil water availability. When soil moisture is below FC, capillary forces dominate over the gravitational forces.

Permanent wilting point (PWP) corresponds to the degree of saturation at which the plants cannot extract water from the soil matrix (i.e., the capillary retention of the soil exceeds the osmotic pressure exerted by the plant roots).

Soil water deficit (SWD) is a metric used to compute the volume of water required to avoid soil moisture in the root zone from dropping below a critical level of saturation where the plant will experience stress conditions. In these conditions, irrigation is required to avoid crop stress and thus a reduction of production yield.

2.3 Groundwater Table

To measure the variations in groundwater table (also referred to as water level or the hydraulic head), a submerged pressure sensor must be placed in an observation well (i.e., piezometer). The variation of water pressure can be used to accurately calculate the elevation of the water table using Eq. 1:

$$h = \frac{p}{\rho g} + z \tag{1}$$

where h is the hydraulic head (m), p is the pressure caused by the water column above the sensor, ρ is the density of water, g is the gravitational force and z is the elevation of the measurement point relative to a reference point (e.g., the sea level). Figure 2 depicts the concept of hydraulic head and associated variables.

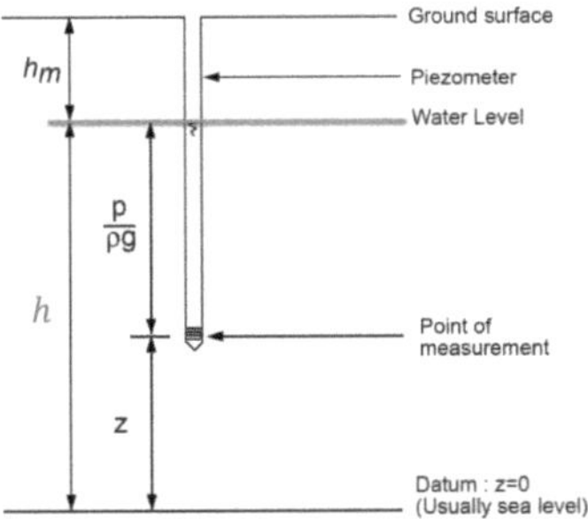

Fig. 2. Concept of the hydraulic head (h).

The measurement of the groundwater table elevation is necessary to accurately represent the effects of capillary rise processes from shallow groundwater levels. The elevation of the water table is typically imposed at the bottom of the soil model.

3 Design

In this section we present the main components and the workflow of the implemented system.

3.1 Environmental Data: Decentlab

Decentlab [8] is a spin off from the Swiss Federal Laboratories for Materials Science and Technology (Empa). They provide low-power environmental sensing solutions used for monitoring meteorological and hydrological variables such as temperature, pressure, and soil moisture. These sensors typically transmit measurements at regular time intervals (i.e., every 15 min they emit one value) producing continuous time-series data streams.

The integration of sensor data enables the hydrological model simulations to be compared with site-specific observations, which must be assimilated to ensure adequate model simulation with respect to local conditions. Note that performing data assimilation (DA) on historical data is out of the scope of this study but can easily be applied with DA-assists framework such as HGS-PDAF [31].

In this paper, we use soil moisture [9] and water pressure sensors [10]. As such, soil and groundwater dynamic states are simultaneously monitored. Moisture probes measure soil moisture in scaled frequency unit (0 = air and 100 = water). Volumetric water content is obtained by applying a generic conversion given by Decentlab. The length of the probe is 60 cm with a sensor every 10 cm (10, 20, 30, 40, 50 and 60 cm). As such, the probe can be vertically installed in the soil, providing a continuous data stream of soil moisture dynamics and pressure. The spatial resolution is fine enough to capture the vertical soil water dynamics in the soil profile. Pressure sensors measure pressure in mbar. Both sensor types are equipped with LoRaWAN© wireless communication and an internal battery. LoRaWAN© is a radio technology enabling encrypted radio transmissions over long distances while consuming very little power [22].

Two probes have been installed on an agricultural plot located in the Seeland agricultural region of Switzerland near the village of Kerzers (Fribourg canton). These two sensors are used in this study to support the development of the IoT-based infrastructure. Moisture sensors are installed directly in the soil and pressure sensors are usually installed in a piezometer. These two remote sensors are measuring soil moisture and water pressure in the piezometer since the 17th of March, 2025. A direct access via secure HTTP API is provided by Decentlab.

3.2   Meteorological Data Sources: MeteoSwiss

MeteoSwiss provides open-access meteorological datasets, including historical observations measured at discrete weather stations and distributed numerical weather forecasts [24]. These datasets offer meteorological information required for environmental modelling applications. In our case, precipitation and PET are the two variables of interest.

The historical dataset is linked to MeteoSwiss' automatic weather stations, while the forecasts are associated with MeteoSwiss' ensemble numerical weather prediction models [25]. As opposed to the historical data, forecast data are continuous over the entire Swiss territory with a resolution of 1 km or 2.1 km, depending on the model. We choose the ICON-CH2-EPS model ensemble. This model ensemble has a horizontal grid size of 2.1 km, contains 21 ensemble members and has a forecast period of 120 h (5 days). For the agricultural application, it is considered that a period of 5 days is enough for predictions of irrigation scheduling. Note that weather forecast uncertainty is increasing with a projected time horizon such that 5 days is an appropriate balance between uncertainty and practicality.

3.3   Hydrological Model: HydroGeoSphere

Rather than focusing on the model, this paper focuses on the database implementation and data collection from different sources. However, because the soil model is used as an application of the developed IoT-based infrastructure, the present section introduces basic elements with respect to the model code and implementation.

HydroGeoSphere (HGS) [2] is a numerical physics-based integrated surface and subsurface hydrological model (ISSHM). Such models solved the state-of-the-art of physics-based equations on a predefined numerical grid (or mesh), discretizing the modelled hydrological system in space.

An integrated hydrological analysis of the hydrological system is accomplished by the coupled solution of the diffusion-wave equation governing 2-D (areal) surface water flow and the Richards' equation governing 3-D unsaturated/saturated subsurface flow [33]. A single system of matrix equations arising from both discretized flow regimes is then assembled for the entire hydrological setting with appropriate boundary conditions being applied to the combined system. The surface and the subsurface flow regimes are coupled following a dual-node approach [20].

The model solves the coupled non-linear equations following the mass-balance conservation approach. For that purpose, the equations are linearized with the Newton-Raphson method [15] and the resulting matrix system is solved iteratively by HGS [4]. The solution is marched through time with an adaptive time-stepping procedure. Because of these necessary numerical steps, the execution of the HGS model is computationally demanding in terms of CPUs. Numerical efficiency can, however, be gained through parallelization of the resolution of the matrix system. However, this is usually only significant for very large (> 100 000 nodes) models.

HGS is widely used in hydrological and hydrogeological communities to analyse groundwater dynamics, surface runoff, and their interactions ([4,5,11,13,32], etc.). Note that HGS can also handle mass transport and heat transfer, however these are outside the scope of this work. An important point is that HGS is not dynamically simulating crop growth processes (i.e., crop models). Rather, crop root depth is imposed. The physiological activity of the plant influencing partitioning of evaporation and transpiration processes can be conceptualized through the application of a crop coefficient approach (see HGS's official documentation [3] for more details).

Implementation of HGS is done following a simple 1D discretization of a soil column with a uniform rectangle of $1m^2$. The conceptualization of the model following a 1D vertical soil column is justified because the variably saturated flow is mostly dominated by vertical flow directions. The top sheet is then replicated at regular intervals of $1\,cm$ down to $1.2\,m$, ensuring a fine discretization of the soil profile. The model is therefore a $1.2\,m$ deep rectangular column with 484 nodes and 120 rectangular elements.

Weather variables (i.e., daily precipitation and daily PET) are imposed fluxes at the top. Recall that the actual ET (AET) computed by the model can be lower than the PET as water stress conditions can occur. Water accumulating at the top of the model can freely leave the model domain through a so-called critical-depth boundary condition. The measured water pressure in the piezometer is used to compute a daily hydraulic head (Eq. 1) imposed at the bottom of the model. The model is therefore forced with daily stress periods.

To simplify the conceptualization of the root depth dynamic, and to support the development of the present IoT-based infrastructure, the maximum root depth is imposed at a fixed depth of 45 cm (potential evapotranspiration flux is therefore distributed along all nodes located within this predefined depth). In our application, the HGS model has usually taken less than 5 min for completion.

3.4   Database: InfluxDB

The datasets used in this work are time-dependent, such as measurements from environmental sensors, historical meteorological data, and outputs from hydrological simulations. These datasets are collected at a daily interval and are always associated with a timestamp.

A time-series database, such as InfluxDB [16], is well-suited for this type of data because it is designed to efficiently store and query large amounts of time-indexed information. It allows fast data ingestion and makes it easy to extract data over specific time windows, e.g., when retrieving the last 30 days of historical data to generate model inputs.

Following the structure of InfluxDB (bucket, measurement, fields and tags), we design specific buckets for each data type. Specifically, Decentlab sensors are stored in the "sensors" bucket. MeteoSwiss historical weather data is stored in the "meteoswiss" bucket. Forecast data from MeteoSwiss and the model outputs are stored in the "forecast" bucket.

3.5   Data Visualisation: Grafana

Grafana [14] is an open-source platform for visualising and monitoring time-series data stored in databases such as InfluxDB. It provides interactive dashboards that support real-time data exploration and aggregation. In this study, we used Grafana to visualise both input data (meteorological, environmental and forecast data) and model outputs stored in the InfluxDB database, without requiring additional post-processing steps.

3.6   Workflow

The overall workflow of the system is shown in Fig. 3. We enumerate each step of the workflow, as indicated directly by the numbers in Fig. 3. The system architecture is composed of two main computing nodes: server A, which hosts the database and the data acquisition components, and server B, which is responsible for running the HydroGeoSphere (HGS) simulations. Communication between both systems is fully automated through a Python script and secure file transfers. Note that data acquisition components and HGS simulations can also be hosted in the same server.

On server A, our Python client executes inside a Docker container. It retrieves the last 30 days of measurement data from physical sensors as well as historical meteorological data provided by MeteoSwiss (① and ③). After processing and formatting, all data are stored in an InfluxDB time-series database (② and ④).

To generate the input files required by HGS, a set of Python scripts on server A prepare both historical and forecast meteorological data. One script retrieves the forecast data from MeteoSwiss, processes it, formats it into the text-file structure (index, value) expected by HGS ⑥. The more recent forecast data are also stored in the database ⑦ as a backup. A second script extracts the last 30 days of historical measurements from the InfluxDB database and writes them to text files in the same input directory ⑨. Note that the length of the historical measurements time-series to extract can easily be adjusted according to the modelling application. However, in the considered soil model application, a time-window of 30 days is sufficient to ensure robust model initialization.

Although these scripts run on server A, they are triggered remotely from server B (⑤ and ⑧) via a secure SSH connection.

Once all required files are available, the script on server B compresses the input directory, and the resulting archive is then transferred from server A to server B, where it is used as the input package for the simulation workflow ⑩. To indicate that the input files are ready, a dummy `ready.txt` file is created. Once the ready file is created, the input files are transferred to a dedicated working directory and the HGS model is automatically executed ⑪ , via a Python script handling all the input data and the model runs. Upon completion, the model generates a new compressed archive containing all simulation outputs and places it in a dedicated output directory ⑫ .

The output archive is then transferred back to server A ⑬ , and decompressed. A post-processing Python script, triggered by the `commander_proxy` file ⑭ , inserts the resulting simulation data into the InfluxDB database ⑮ . We leverage Graphana to visualize all time series via easy to read dashboards ⑯ .

4   Implementation

We implemented our prototype in Python (v3.0). We used Docker [12] to deploy the database, data retrieval scripts and for visualisation. On server A, we used separate containers for the InfluxDB database and for the data acquisition and preprocessing through Python scripts. We leverage Docker Compose to create and orchestrate containers, also to facilitate network configuration, volume mappings, and service dependencies. The architecture uses persistent storage volumes to ensure that the database is not affected in case of container restarts. The

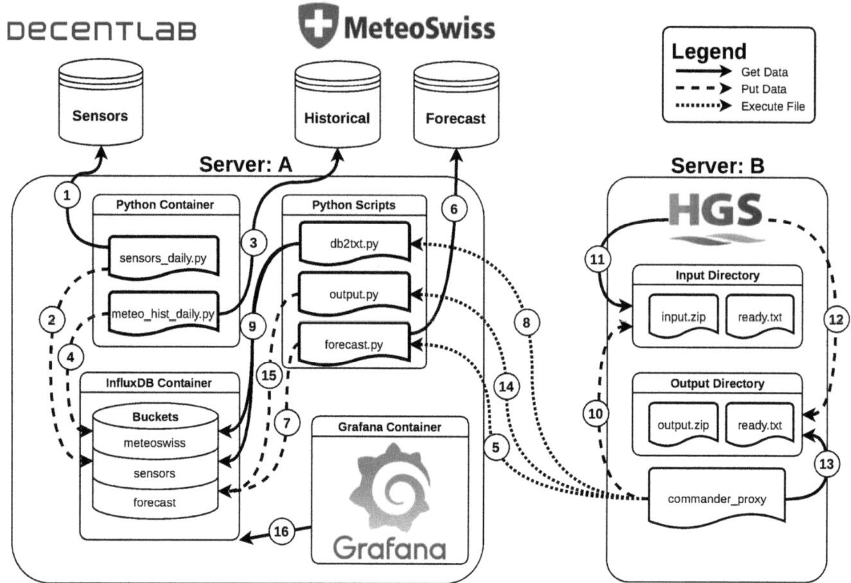

Fig. 3. Schematic of the IoT-based infrastructure.

database container is constructed from the `influxdb:2-alpine` image [17]. Writing and access is done with the `influxdb_client` Python library. The Python container is constructed on the `python:3` image [28], and naturally depends on a proper initialization of the database container. The automation part of the system is done with the `schedule` Python package. It enables to schedule jobs at certain times of the day.

4.1   Data Acquisition and Preprocessing

Each type of data (sensors, historical from MeteoSwiss and forecast from MeteoSwiss) is acquired through a dedicated Python script. These scripts run on a daily basis and store the historical meteorological data into the database. Decentlab procures Python bindings supporting few functions facilitating the retrieval of data from the sensors. The data is sorted and filtered before being stored in the database. Only pressures greater than 0.01 mbar and moisture values greater than 1 SFU are being considered. MeteoSwiss provides direct access to its historical data through a public REST API . The format of the data is a CSV file that is read using the `pandas` package. Daily time series from January 1st of this year until yesterday are downloaded and the last value is added to the database. This python script is scheduled to run every day at 5:01 UTC; this was chosen to ensure that MeteoSwiss updates (in between 2:00 UTC and 3:00 UTC) are completed.

Forecast data are retrieved automatically before each simulation run. Precipitation data can be downloaded directly while potential evapotranspiration (PET) can be calculated as follows [27]:

$$PET = \frac{0.4}{30}(23.9R_s + 50)(\frac{T}{T + 15}) \tag{2}$$

where R_s is the global radiation in $[MJm^{-2}d^{-1}]$ and T is the daily mean temperature in $[°C]$.

Preprocessing the data includes temporal and spatial resampling, unit normalisation, and formatting into text-based input files. For spatial resampling, the 4 nearest grid points are averaged with a distance based pondered mean. We rely on existing third-party Python libraries to calculate the distance between two points using Harvesine method [23].

4.2   Communication Between Servers

In our experimental setup, establishing a direct connection between the two considered servers was challenging due to their different security constraints. One server is accessible only through an internal network or via a Virtual Private Network (VPN). The other requires access through a proxy jump. These restrictions imposed limitations on direct data exchange. Initially, the objective was to access server **B** directly from server **A**, but this approach was impossible due to the network configuration. As a result, the workflow was changed so that all data transfers are initiated from server **B** instead. To manage these transfers, a Python control script was implemented using the **paramiko** and **paramiko_jump** libraries. This script handles both the retrieval of input files from server **A** and the return of simulation output files back to server **A**.

4.3   Visualisation and Monitoring

To visualise both input data and simulation results, we leverage Grafana as a visualisation layer connected to the InfluxDB database. Predefined dashboards are configured to display time series from sensor measurements, meteorological data, and HydroGeoSphere outputs.

Dashboards include panels for variables such as precipitation, temperature, and pressure, allowing the users to have a real-time visualisation of the database. Using Grafana's support for fine-grain customization, one can filter data on a time basis, enabling flexible visualisation of different simulation periods.

5   Results

In this section, we present first the historical data gathered since the sensors have been deployed and started collecting measurements. Subsequently, we present the simulation results obtained from the application of the HGS model. The whole workflow (i.e., data transfer and model run) requires less that 4 min to execute.

Obtaining the forecast data takes around 1 min and 40 s and model simulation around 1 min and 30 s. For all the other steps, less than 3 s are required. These execution times are fully compatible with the present workflow for near real-time application.

5.1   Historical Data

Historical data pertaining to sensors and meteorological variables are shown in Fig. 4. As it is expected for shallow depths, an increase in soil moisture correlates with precipitation events. Depending on the different depths, the soil moisture time series are not similar. This illustrates the dynamic behaviours of the soil profile. In wet conditions (i.e., from September to February), high soil moisture measurements are associated with the top and bottom horizons of the soil profile, while low soil moisture values are found in between. This is probably linked to the proximity of the groundwater level (capillary fringe) and low evapotranspiration processes. In dry conditions (i.e., from March to August), lowest soil moisture measurements are more tightened altogether along depth, indicating a more uniform vertical distribution of soil moisture. This is probably because less water is percolating through the soil horizons due to increased evapotranspiration demands. In this use-case paper, the last 30 days of the historical data (precipitation and evapotranspiration) are used to properly initialize the dynamic state of modelled soil moisture in the considered soil column.

5.2   Model Simulations

The HGS model is forced with 35 days, including 30 days of historical data and 5 days of forecasts (i.e., 21 ensemble members from the ICON-CH2-EPS model ensemble). Note that historical soil moisture is not considered, as data assimilation is not performed. Model simulations are, therefore, pure forward model runs with default soil parameter values. Soil moisture model simulations are shown in Fig. 5. During the historical period, all the 21 members are similar because the same historical weather forcings are used. Differences observed in the forecast period are therefore directly related to the variance in the input data from the ICON-CH2-EPS model ensemble.

From soil moisture simulations, the soil water deficit (SWD) can be calculated (Fig. 5). Recall that negative values indicate no specific water stress conditions. For the considered forecast period, the soil has enough water to sustain transpiration from the plants. For the same reasons as soil moisture, variance in the calculated SWD is observed only during the forecast period.

6   Conclusion and Future Work

This paper introduces a novel application that couples an IoT-based infrastructure with a mechanistic soil model designed to account for shallow groundwater levels and capillary rise processes in an agricultural water management context.

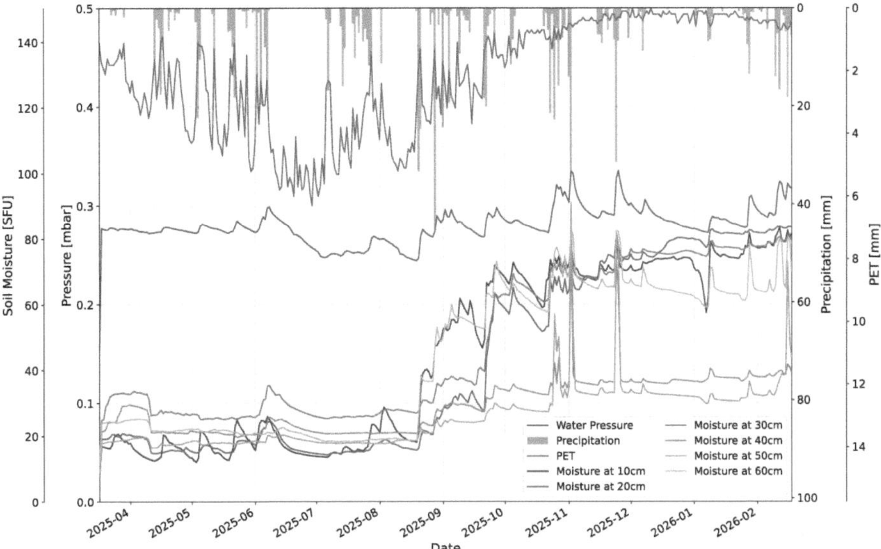

Fig. 4. Time series (2025) of soil moisture probe (id:22989) consisting of 6 soil moisture sensors. Note that moisture is not in percent but in scaled frequency unit (SFU): 0 corresponds to a dried out soil, and 100 to full saturation. Soil moisture is measured at depths of 10,20,30,40,50, and 60 cm.

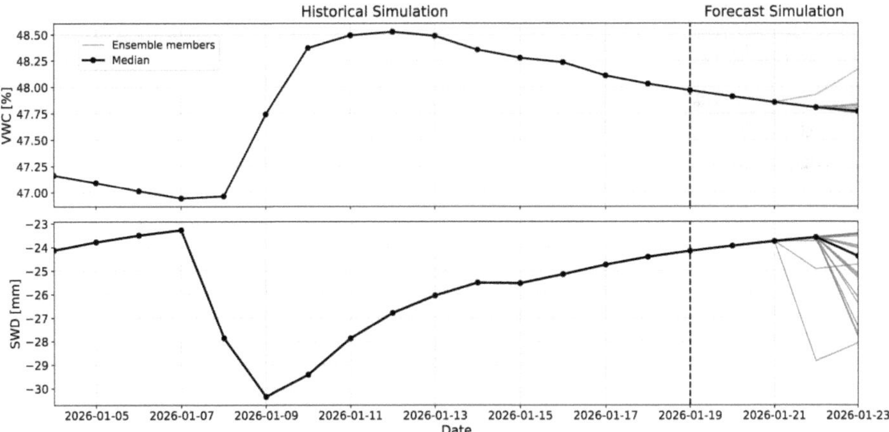

Fig. 5. Volumetric water content (VWC; top panel) and modelled soil water deficits (SWD; bottom panel) encompassing a historical and forecast period. Note that the variance in the forecast period is only due to the variance in the input weather data.

Our framework is automated on a daily basis, accounting for recent historical data and updated weather forecasts to be included in a centralized database. The implemented IoT-based infrastructure successfully undertakes data collection from various data providers and generates relevant input files for the model application. In an agricultural water management context, soil water deficits are computed from simulated soil moisture for the next 5 days. These short-term forecasts can provide a basis to guide agricultural water management practices regarding irrigation needs. Simulation results are transferred back to a centralized database, which can be used as a source for visualisation. The workflow successfully integrates multiple systems and software components and real-life testbeds (i.e., Decentlab, HGS and MeteoSwiss), showcasing efficient operations.

By expanding the modelling capacity to the explicit representation of groundwater capillary rise processes, the robustness of the modelling framework to simulate dynamic soil moisture conditions in shallow groundwater environments is improved. More complex models can also be considered to simulate, for instance, regional-scale groundwater table levels updated on a regular basis. This can open new opportunities for managing water resources at the regional scale, enabling the joint management of surface and subsurface water resources.

Future Work. Implementation of data assimilation to this IoT-based infrastructure is needed to provide consistent forecasts with respect to local conditions. The IoT-based infrastructure was developed with an agricultural-based application but is not restricted to. Other water management applications involving dynamic updates such as estimation of groundwater recharge or time-varying wellhead protection zones can also be addressed in a near real-time.

Acknowledgements. The authors acknowledge the funding received through the SNSF BRIDGE Discovery project grant #218621.

References

1. Allan, R., Pereira, L., Smith, M.: Crop evapotranspiration-Guidelines for computing crop water requirements-FAO Irrigation and drainage paper 56, vol. 56, FAO - Food and Agriculture Organization of the United Nations (1998)
2. Aquanty: HydroGeoSphere. https://www.aquanty.com/hydrogeosphere
3. Aquanty: HydroGeoSphere Documentation (latest) (2026). https://docs.aquanty.com/en/latest/. Accessed 21 Feb 2026
4. Brunner, P., Simmons, C.: HydroGeoSphere: a fully integrated, physically based hydrological model. Ground Water **50**, 170–6 (2011). https://doi.org/10.1111/j.1745-6584.2011.00882.x
5. Callaghan, M., et al.: Development of a fully integrated hydrological fate and transport model for plant protection products: incorporating groundwater, tile drainage, and runoff. Front. Environ. Sci. **12** (2024). https://doi.org/10.3389/fenvs.2024.1505480
6. Confédération Suisse: federal office of meteorology and climatology MeteoSwiss. https://www.meteoswiss.admin.ch
7. Confédération Suisse: Adaptation aux changements climatiques en suisse. plan d'action 2020–2025. Office fédéral de l'environnement, p. 164 (2020)
8. Decentlab: Decentlab. https://www.decentlab.com

9. Decentlab GmbH: DL-SMTP: Soil moisture and temperature profile for LoRaWAN® (2025). https://www.decentlab.com/products/soil-moisture-and-temperature-profile-for-lorawan, product page. Accessed 09 Apr 2026

10. Decentlab GmbH: High-Precision Pressure / Liquid Level and Temperature Sensor for LoRaWAN® (2025). https://www.decentlab.com/products/high-precision-pressure-/-liquid-level-and-temperature-sensor-for-lorawan. reference DL-PR36, product page. Accessed 09 Apr 2026

11. Delottier, H., Therrien, R., Young, N., Paradis, D.: A hybrid approach for integrated surface and subsurface hydrologic simulation of baseflow with iterative ensemble smoother. J. Hydrol. **606**, 127406 (2021). https://doi.org/10.1016/j.jhydrol.2021.127406

12. Docker: What is docker? https://docs.docker.com/get-started/docker-overview/

13. Gong, C., Cook, P., Therrien, R., Wang, W., Brunner, P.: On groundwater recharge in variably saturated subsurface flow models. Water Resour. Res. **59** (2023). https://doi.org/10.1029/2023WR034920

14. Grafana Labs: Grafana (2026). https://grafana.com/oss/grafana/. Accessed 09 Apr 2026

15. Huyakorn, P.S., Pinder, G.F.: Computational Methods in Subsurface Flow. Academic Press, New York (1983)

16. InfluxData: Get started with InfluxDB | InfluxDB OSS v2 documentation (2026). https://docs.influxdata.com/influxdb/v2/get-started/, documentation page. Accessed 09 Apr 2026

17. InfluxData: InfluxDB docker official image. https://hub.docker.com/_/influxdb (2026), official image on Docker Hub. Accessed 09 Apr 2026

18. Kroes, J., Supit, I., Van Dam, J., Van Walsum, P., Mulder, M.: Impact of capillary rise and recirculation on simulated crop yields. Hydrol. Earth Syst. Sci. **22**(5), 2937–2952 (2018)

19. Li, W., et al.: Potential evaporation dynamics over saturated bare soil and an open water surface. J. Hydrol. **590**, 125140 (2020). https://doi.org/10.1016/j.jhydrol.2020.125140

20. Liggett, J.E., Werner, A.D., Simmons, C.T.: Influence of the first-order exchange coefficient on simulation of coupled surface-subsurface flow. J. Hydrol. **414**, 503–515 (2012)

21. Loconsole, D., Elia, M., Conversa, G., De Lucia, B., Cristiano, G., Elia, A.: Soil moisture sensing technologies: principles, applications, and challenges in agriculture. Agronomy **15**, 2788 (2025). https://doi.org/10.3390/agronomy15122788

22. LoRa Alliance: About LoRaWAN® (2026). https://lora-alliance.org/about-lorawan/, web page. Accessed 09 Apr 2026

23. Mapado: Haversine. https://github.com/mapado/haversine

24. MeteoSwiss: Open data documentation. https://opendatadocs.meteoswiss.ch

25. MeteoSwiss: Numerical weather forecasting model icon-ch1/2-eps (2026). https://opendatadocs.meteoswiss.ch/e-forecast-data/e2-e3-numerical-weather-forecasting-model, open Data Documentation. Accessed 09 Apr 2026

26. OFEV (éd.): Eaux suisses. État et mesures. Office fédéral de l'environnement (2207), 93 (2022)

27. Pierluigi Calanca, Pascalle Smith, A.H.e.C.A.: L'évapotranspiration de référence et son application en agrométéorologie. Recherche Agronomique Suisse (2011). https://doi.org/10.48550/arXiv.2208.13982

28. Python: Docker hub: python. https://hub.docker.com/_/python/

29. Simmons, C.T., Brunner, P., Therrien, R., Sudicky, E.A.: Commemorating the 50th anniversary of the Freeze and Harlan (1969) blueprint for a physically-based, digitally-simulated hydrologic response model. J. Hydrol. **584**, 124309 (2020)
30. Sushanth, G., Sujatha, S.: IoT based smart agriculture system. In: 2018 International Conference on Wireless Communications, Signal Processing and Networking (WiSPNET), pp. 1–4. IEEE (2018)
31. Tang, Q., Delottier, H., Kurtz, W., Nerger, L., Schilling, O.S., Brunner, P.: HGS-PDAF (version 1.0): a modular data assimilation framework for an integrated surface and subsurface hydrological model. Geosci. Model Dev **17**(8), 3559–3578 (2024). https://doi.org/10.5194/gmd-17-3559-2024
32. Tang, Q., Schilling, O.S., Kurtz, W., Brunner, P., Vereecken, H., Hendricks Franssen, H.J.: Simulating flood-induced riverbed transience using unmanned aerial vehicles, physically based hydrological modeling, and the ensemble Kalman filter. Water Resour. Res. **54**(11), 9342–9363 (2018). https://doi.org/10.1029/2018WR023067
33. Vereecken, H., et al.: Modeling soil processes: review, key challenges, and new perspectives. Vadose Zone J. 15(5), vzj2015-09 (2016)
34. Zipper, S.C., Soylu, M.E., Booth, E.G., Loheide, S.P.: Untangling the effects of shallow groundwater and soil texture as drivers of subfield-scale yield variability. Water Resour. Res. **51**(8), 6338–6358 (2015)

Author Index